ACROSS  PLAINS

SARAH ROYCE

ACROSS  PLAINS

SARAH ROYCE'S WESTERN NARRATIVE

Edited by
JENNIFER DAWES ADKISON

The University of Arizona Press
Tucson

The University of Arizona Press
© 2009 The Arizona Board of Regents
All rights reserved

www.uapress.arizona.edu

Library of Congress Cataloging-in-Publication Data
Royce, Sarah, 1819–1891.
Across the Plains : Sarah Royce's western narrative / Sarah Royce ;
edited by Jennifer Dawes Adkison.
p. cm. — (Women's western voices)
Sarah Royce's memoirs, written in the 1880's, of her trip across
the Plains to California in 1849.
Includes bibliographical references and index.
ISBN 978-0-8165-2726-7 (pbk. : acid-free paper)
1. Royce, Sarah, 1819–1891. 2. Overland journeys to the Pacific. 3. Frontier
and pioneer life—California. 4. Women pioneers—California–Biography. 5.
California—Gold discoveries. I. Adkison, Jennifer Dawes, 1966– II. Title.
F865.R857 2009
917.804'2—dc22

2009003101

Publication of this book is made possible in part by
the proceeds of a permanent endowment created with
the assistance of a Challenge Grant from the National
Endowment for the Humanities, a federal agency.

♻

Manufactured in the United States of America on acid-free,
archival-quality paper containing a minimum of 30% post-consumer
waste and processed chlorine free.

14   13   12   11   10   09   6   5   4   3   2   1

Book composition: David Alcorn, Alcorn Publication Design

·:· ·:· ·:·
Contents

❖ ❖ ❖
Acknowledgments

This project (or rather the idea for it) began nearly ten years ago, when, as a graduate student of English at University of Nevada, Reno, I proposed to write a dissertation chapter on Sarah Royce's narrative. Committee member and historian Scott Casper asked the question, "Where is the manuscript?" I had to admit at the time that I did not know, that I had not even considered how the manuscript could be useful, essential even, to my planned project.

Fortunately for me at the time, the manuscript was just a few hours down the road at the Bancroft Library. Viewing Royce's handwritten manuscript for the first time was an unexpected pleasure. Realizing how much of her narrative had never been published inspired me to pursue this work.

Looking back now ten years later, I am grateful to Scott for his question because it has led to the volume you now hold in your hands. I am also appreciative of the early support and encouragement that I received from my friends and mentors at UNR, notably Cheryll Glotfelty, Mike Branch, and Ann Ronald.

My work on this book was supported in part by a grant from the Idaho Humanities Council, a State-Based Program of the National Endowment for the Humanities. I am also deeply appreciative of the financial support from the Faculty Research Committee at Idaho State University, without which this book could not have been completed. The photo of Sarah Royce by Fannie L. Matson is reproduced courtesy of the Department of Special Collections, Charles E. Young Research Library, UCLA.

I want to thank Nancy Wall for her eagle-eyed proofreading, Laura Woodworth-Ney for believing in this project all along, and my students here at ISU for inspiring me with their enthusiasm and interest in my work.

Like Sarah Royce, I value the support of a loving family—my spouse, Steve, and children, Bridger, Ally, and Jacob. I would also like to acknowledge the support of my parents, Jim and Barbara Dawes, for child care and other assistance in crisis situations, most particularly my mother to whom my work on this book is lovingly dedicated.

ACROSS THE PLAINS

Sarah Royce in about 1890. (Courtesy of the Department of Special Collections, Charles E. Young Research
Library, UCLA)

INTRODUCTION
Authorship, Authenticity and the Gold Rush West

Jennifer Dawes Adkison

"The morning of that 30th of April was not very bright; but neither was it very gloomy. Rain might come within an hour, but then the sun might come out,—I would not consent to delay our departure for fear of the weather. Had I not made up my mind to encounter many storms? If we were going, let us go, and meet what we were to meet bravely."[1] In this brief passage at the beginning of her narrative, Sarah Royce alludes to the unknowns she and her family face and the spirit, resolve, and determination it will take to meet the challenge. In this declaration, she also constructs herself in the image of the brave pioneer woman whose fortitude and strength provided the foundation for early California history. Scholars of western history and literature have long used her words to form a representative and iconic vision of the resolute pioneer woman.[2] No one, however, has yet considered Royce's own self-conscious creation of this persona. The persona she creates in her writing, coupled with her claims for the authenticity of her story and for her own authority to tell it, reveal much about Royce's view of her own authorial role and situate her firmly within the context of western authorship.

Reflecting back from thirty years after her pioneer experience, Royce not only writes of the struggle and hardship she encountered on the trail, she also comments upon her own position as an eyewitness to the events that shaped western American history. In doing so, she joins numerous other writers of "pioneer reminiscences" in recounting the past in order to shape the present understanding of the early settlers and their contribution to the fabric of

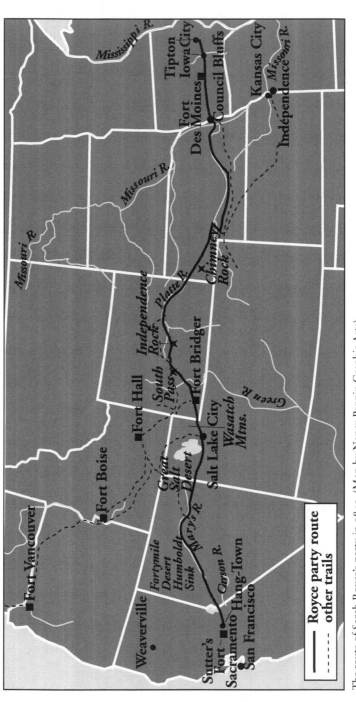

The route of Sarah Royce's party in 1849. (Map by Nancy Peppin Graphic Arts)

western society. In order to fully understand what Royce is doing in her memoir, one must consider that her account is not simply an accurate reflection of what happened but a version of experience crafted to reveal Royce's own belief in the fundamental role of spiritual fervor and religious faith as foundations of society. In *Promised Lands*, historian David Wrobel writes that "Promotional tracts and pioneer reminiscences are thoroughly unreliable as objective gauges of 'past reality' (itself a slippery phenomenon) because they were produced for very definite purposes; yet all historical sources are, in some degree, the products of purposeful creation."[3] Wrobel concludes that "The pioneers' purposefully created selective memories were intended to ensure that their authors' roles in history would not be forgotten in the present or the future. . . . Older generations of westerners were trying to maintain their status in a changing West by reminding younger generations of the pivotal role they had played in the past."[4] Like the pioneers of whom Wrobel writes, Royce presents her own primacy and connection to the important experiences and events that were becoming, at the time of her writing in the 1880s, icons of the western story. In doing so, her purpose is to project a world in which spiritual faith and values shape and guide every action and interaction.

In considering the circumstances of her early years, it seems improbable that a woman like Sarah Royce would become an icon of western womanhood. Royce is not unlike so many of the women who went west in the mid-nineteenth century, however. The very aspects of her life that made her genteel and refined contrasted with the stamina and perseverance necessary for the westward trek. In *Roaring Camp*, historian Susan Lee Johnson considers how the event—the California Gold Rush—"has been construed more and more narrowly over time until it has come to connote merely fast fortune."[5] Johnson takes exception to this portrayal and encourages us to consider the "alternative plot lines, stories not customarily nourished by the dominant culture, broadly defined, or even by most historical scholarship."[6] In keeping with Johnson's remarks, Royce's story has the potential of being generalized to become the western woman's story. It is easy to see Royce as the generic stalwart pioneer woman and in doing so to fail to hear Royce herself speak as her voice gets lost in our own interpretation of her words. Royce's story offers us one of those alternate plot lines, however—a story decidedly not motivated by "fast fortune."

A close examination of Royce's life story reveals a woman who could not, by her own admission, have been less fit to make the overland journey at midcentury. Claiming never to have even camped out before, Royce encounters harsh and unforgiving environments both on the trail and in California, with no shelter but the canvas covering the family's wagon or the flimsy walls of a makeshift tent home. Royce's early years were spent in middle-class comfort in urban environments. In her narrative she tells the story of a "lady" thrust into a world that challenged her own gendered assumptions about her role. Johnson writes, "The West is historically a place of disrupted gender relations and stunning racial and ethnic diversity, a diversity structured by inequality and injustice."[7] Instead of having this experience sway Royce's beliefs about herself and her role—"disrupting" her own conceptions about how and where she fits into the world—Royce self-consciously uses this disjuncture to show a woman being tested and persevering while maintaining her sense of self. It is this testing, she claims, that refined her faith, her writing, and her life into the image that she consciously presents in her narrative, that of the stalwart pioneer.

Despite her compelling experience, the world might not know much at all about Sarah Royce if it were not for her son, the influential Harvard philosopher Josiah Royce, who in 1880 requested that she write the story of her life on the overland trail and in early California. What little we can learn about Royce's early years must be gleaned largely from the work of historians and biographers whose scholarly interest in Sarah Royce has focused upon Josiah Royce's early home life and parentage in an effort to reveal early insights into the development of his philosophy. We do know that Sarah Eleanor Bayliss was born on March 2, 1819, in Stratford-upon-Avon, England. As a baby of only three months, she was brought by her parents to live alternately in Germantown, Pennsylvania, and New York City, until they finally settled in Rochester, New York, when Sarah was nine. There she eventually met and married her husband, Josiah Sr.

It was as a girl and young woman in a time and place characterized by religious zeal that she developed the strong faith that she leans on throughout her narrative.[8] Her actual religious affiliation seems to have wavered between the Congregationalist Church and the Disciples of Christ. Josiah Royce Jr.'s biographer John Clendenning notes that she preferred the Congregationalists to the more evangelical Disciples. Josiah Sr., however, joined the Disciples of Christ in 1857, and by 1859 he and Sarah had helped to organize a congregation of this denomination in Grass Valley. In fact, it is in her early years that the two common themes of Sarah's narrative—mobility for economic advancement and the tenacious hold of spiritual faith and values—were established in her life. Clendenning writes of the upstate New York region where Sarah Royce grew up and its importance in shaping her religious faith and philosophy of life: "During the first half of the nineteenth century, the upstate region of New York—like California during the latter half of the century—was boisterously transitional."[9] The completion of the Erie Canal in 1825 stimulated development and economic growth. Because of the social transformation and religious upheaval of the area, it came to be known as the Burned-Over District—so named by historian Whitney R. Cross to represent the intense flames of spirituality that had consumed the area. New religions were founded; Joseph Smith uncovered the Book of Mormon in Palmyra, New York and later founded the Church of Jesus Christ of Latter-Day Saints. Utopian societies, including the Shakers and the Owenites, prospered. What is notable about this time and place in relation to Royce's story is the social confusion that served as a backdrop to her early years—the struggle between old and new, and between the establishment and those elements that threatened the established beliefs, mores, and ways of life. The young woman who emerged from this place knew where she stood. One of the few books Royce brought west with her was the Bible.

Royce was well educated for a woman of her day. A graduate of Phipps Union Female Seminary in Albion, New York, she was trained in the domestic arts of etiquette and housewifery but also studied more academic subjects that fit her for her chosen profession of teacher. After finishing her own formal schooling, she seems to have embraced the role of teacher and worked as an educator throughout her life in various capacities in her home and in public schools. Each of her own children spent their early years being educated by their mother.

By the time she married her husband, Josiah, Sarah Royce quite likely had already begun to form what would become her refined sense of herself and her place in the world. In contrast, Josiah Sr. seems to have struggled with direction and purpose. Historian Robert V. Hine characterizes him as "the man who never prospered but at least persisted."[10] Throughout their lives—and particularly in the early years of their marriage—this lack of prosperity and constant seeking of it caused the Royces to pick up stakes and move. By the time they settled in Grass Valley in 1854, they had moved nine times in the less than five years that they had been in California.[11] When viewed within this context of mobility and transience, Sarah Royce's insistence in her narrative on the moral imperatives of social conduct and ethical behavior can be seen as a way of coping with the family's constant upheavals, of bringing order to an experience that was characterized by uncertainty.

Three years after their marriage in 1845, the Royces, along with their daughter, Mary Eleanor, who had been born in 1846, moved to a village near Tipton, Iowa, which they almost certainly saw as a jumping-off point for their eventual westward journey.[12] Interestingly enough, at this point the Royces probably had no knowledge of the impending Gold Rush. Clendenning writes: "The Royces were certainly established in Iowa when they first heard of the gold strike, for rumors of the discovery did not reach the East until August, and not until December were they officially confirmed in the president's message to Congress."[13] The news of the gold strike may have spurred them to action and encouraged their progress, but Royce does not discuss their reasons for moving west or whether she herself wanted to go. As they pull out of Tipton on April 30, 1849, Royce characterizes herself as one who is determined to make the trip successfully: "Had I not made up my mind to encounter many storms? If we were going, let us go, and meet what we were to meet bravely" (1). In the opening pages of her story, she begins the creation of a persona that has come to exemplify strength and vision.

The narrative Royce created out of the diary she kept on the trail and her recollections of life in California spans nearly thirty-five and a half years. Key to understanding Royce's story is the idea that her narrative is not strictly a representation of historical and personal events; it is also a meditation on these occurrences and their larger significance, and a spiritual autobiography of a woman discovering the depth of her own faith. Vincent Buranelli writes: "Sarah Royce was not just writing autobiography. She was expounding a philosophy of life, a religion to which she went for consolation during the trek."[14] Beginning with their departure on April 30, 1849, and concluding on September 9, 1884, with her return to the house where they first resided in San Francisco, the narrative leaves out many of the family's experiences and only alludes to others, like the birth of their children—Harriette in 1850, Ruth in 1853, and Josiah Jr. in 1855. John Samuel, who was born in 1852 and died as an infant, is not mentioned specifically. Exact dates and precise details of events related to her own and her husband's employment are not typically named, but one does get a sense in the narrative of the mobility and transience of the Royces as they move from one mining camp to the next and reside variously in Sacramento, San Francisco, and Grass Valley. In fact, Josiah Sr.'s assorted business ventures often kept him away from home—a fact that Sarah Royce notes quite ruefully in her narrative. All his life he seemed to strive for a place of financial comfort, if not wealth, that was just beyond his grasp. With the help of Sarah, Josiah Sr. worked as a grocer and shopkeeper in the mining camps and a fruit vendor in the San Francisco area. If Sarah was bitter about their financial failings, in her narrative she holds her tongue. Through all of their trials and hardships, the woman who emerges in her narrative is one who persists and moves on.

Sarah Royce as Western Author

Long viewed by scholars as a classic example of western narrative written by a Gold Rush woman, Royce's story seems upon first glance to be just that. Early scholars of western women's narratives focused on their role as civilizers of the "wild" frontier, and previous scholarship has portrayed Royce as the quintessential culture bearer.[15] It is easy to read her narrative as such because Royce's overt moralizing tends to cast her in this role. A closer study of Royce's narrative, however, reveals the complexity of her portrayal and suggests that there are two contexts within which to consider her story: the overt one, a tale of a mother writing her life at the request of and for the benefit of her son, and the understory, which reveals and argues, sometimes insistently, that Royce was a *writer* using rhetorical strategies to emphasize the importance of her perspective as an eyewitness to the events she depicts. When viewed together, these two stories provide us with a clearer picture of Royce, her narrative, and its significance to western studies.

Early scholarship on Royce focused on her supporting role as mother to her well-known son and his role in interpreting California history and ignored issues of authority and authorship.[16] However, her narrative, previously published as *A Frontier Lady: Recollections of the Gold Rush and Early California*, has become for many scholars one of the preeminent texts on women and the Gold Rush, and she has most often been read as a kind of stereotypical "western woman"—a familiar image in western history and literary studies. Scholars have suggested that the dearth of published women's narratives from the Gold Rush makes the Royce narrative a particularly important document. Royce's narrative is certainly important for the information she provides about women's lives on the trail. But if we move beyond the role of her text as simply an historical artifact, we can begin to consider the ways she uses and interprets the genre of the western narrative.

Historically, the problem has been that Royce's authority gets lost in both the context for and editing of the previous edition of her work and in the stereotypes that have pervaded the study of western women. Early scholarly work on western women's experiences and literary production focused on their role as culture bearers, bringing civilization to a rough and unready new world.[17] More recent examinations of women's lives in the West have questioned this construction and have offered a multiplicity of visions of women's roles in the West.[18] In the fields of western history and literary criticism, scholars have moved beyond reclaiming texts like Royce's to considering them within a broader and more complex context. Literary critic Susan H. Swetnam claims that the study of western women's writing has become "arguably one of the centers of gravity in the field of western American studies."[19] In a recent review essay, Swetnam urges other western literary scholars to carefully consider the complex nature of western women's narratives and scholarly interpretations of them. "We can't allow ourselves to reach programmatically for predictable conclusions," she writes, "substituting our own stereotypes for traditional ones. We must be courageous in acknowledging the complexity of our subject matter; we mustn't allow ourselves to be led by our rhetoric or by our assumptions, but by the primary material that we examine."[20] Similarly, in 2005 historian Anne M. Butler wrote about the shifts in the study of western women's history: "Energized by earlier works that established the legitimacy of studying the women's West, current research turns on issues of bias and culture, resistance and strategy, negotiation and accommodation, sexuality and power, womanhood, manhood, and personhood to understand the tangled humanity of the old and the new West."[21] Butler's and Swetnam's words suggest that current scholarship in both western history and literary criticism should move beyond the reconsideration of western women's stereotypes to the considered engagement in the larger ongoing critical conversation on these women and their work.

In order to engage in this conversation, scholars need accessible editions of western women's narratives. In the case of Sarah Royce, the editing of her manuscript in the previous edition of her work and scholars' reliance on this version have problematized the portrayal of Royce. Five sections of Royce's manuscript were excised in the first edition of her narrative, and her continuous writing was shaped into chapters by editor Ralph Henry Gabriel. The deleted sections range in length from a single paragraph to several pages and include Royce's original conclusion and an interesting and potentially damning story about a married woman in California whose husband mistreats her and frequently leaves her on her own to fend for herself. This story, written in response to public opinion that bachelors were insinuating themselves into the hearts of married women, is followed by a note in the text, identified as the handwriting of Sarah's daughter Ruth, that the four pages that would have followed have been removed from the manuscript. The contents of these four pages and their whereabouts (if they still exist) are a mystery that no one has yet to note as there is no reference to them in the previous edition. Nevertheless, the parts of her text that were not included in the previous edition give us a fuller picture of Sarah Royce. Further, the editorial decision to break the manuscript into chapters and to give each chapter a title has led literary scholars to make erroneous claims about the narrative that cannot be substantiated by Royce's actual text.[22] All of these changes are particularly important from a literary perspective as they distort our understanding of the choices that Royce herself made in presenting her story.

In order to fully understand the rhetorical strategies Royce uses to underscore her own authority and the authenticity of her text, we must first consider the larger context in which she was writing. In 1884, hard at work on his history of California, Josiah requested that his mother write her memoirs of life on the overland trail and in early California. He intended to use his mother's experience as source material for his study that would be published as a part of Houghton Mifflin's American Commonwealth series.[23] In the 1880s, recognizing the significance of the historical era of which they had been a part, a number of '49ers had begun to inscribe their memories into the history of California. Michael Kowalewski describes the impulse felt by participants in the Gold Rush to comprehend and chronicle what they knew to be a significant historical moment: "The Gold Rush embodied America's new sense of itself as mirrored in California, whether the image reflected back was seen as a triumphal exemplification of sun-burned American know-how or as a cautionary tale about monetary greed and xenophobia only seventy-five years after the Declaration of Independence. Debated and pondered at the time, the precise significance of the Gold Rush remained (and still remains) open to question."[24]

In the opening lines of *California*, Josiah Royce claims that his dual purpose is to "help the reader towards an understanding of two things: namely, the modern American State of California, and our national character as displayed in that land."[25] It was the larger significance of the history of California that so engrossed Josiah Royce that what he originally conceived as a kind of side project turned into a three-year, multi-city research endeavor. Royce was intrigued by the significance of California to the nation. In discussing Josiah's decision to research and write his history, Kevin Starr notes, "In one brief decade California had replayed on a representative scale the entire course of American history, from discovery to crisis to social cohesion. The nation of 1886 had much to learn from the experience of the 1846–56 California frontier."[26] Historians contemporary with Royce also sought to understand the development of their state—most notably Hubert Howe Bancroft, who collected and edited extensive materials in his *History of California* and whose chief writer, Henry Lebbeus Oak, mentored Josiah in his own research.[27] Sarah Royce faithfully recorded her experiences for her son, but as she did, it is probable that she herself would have been aware of the larger significance of her own story not only to the scholarship of her son but also to the larger historical record.

It is possible—perhaps likely—that at the time they migrated in 1849 Sarah Royce understood the significance, both at a personal level and for the nation, of the vast westward movement of which she and her family would be a part.[28] On the trail, Royce recorded the daily events of life in her "Pilgrim's Diary." She used this trail diary as source material for her own narrative, freely quoting from it in her writing and referring to it as a memory prompt about events from thirty years before.[29] Like her son, Sarah Royce shows awareness in her writing of participating in the great significance of this period for California history, as scholars have noted. Brigitte Georgi-Findlay contextualizes Royce's narrative with the writings of other women in the 1880s who felt compelled by contemporary interest in the earlier "frontier" days to write their stories: "By the 1880s, a regional interest in the pioneer past had developed, giving rise to the writing of pioneer histories and reminiscences of overland travel and early frontier life in the Far West, among them the previously discussed reminiscences of Sarah Royce, Catharine Haun, and Sarah Raymond Herndon."[30] If Josiah Royce was an official chronicler of California history, then his mother provided the underlying story line from which to hang his own narrative, as both participated in a larger cultural phenomenon to reexamine and retell the past.

Recent critical conversations about authenticity and the West suggest the importance of considering the "understory" of Royce's narrative—that of the intentional mythmaker—and the role of mythmaking in constructing her story. Nathaniel Lewis claims that "if, as others have argued, authorship for eastern writers increasingly emphasized the individualized authorial personality and imaginative genius, authorship in the West revolved first around the perceived *authenticity* of the work and *authority* of the writer, and second around any internal 'interest' of the text."[31] In his book *Unsettling the Literary West*, Lewis asks several key questions that could be productively applied to Royce and her narrative: "What happens when the claim of authenticity is examined critically and is revealed to be not only a quixotic rhetorical strategy but also a form of authorial self-invention? What happens when the repeated claims of authenticity are themselves treated as constituting a narrative of literary history? And what happens to western literature when it is unhinged from authenticity—from history, from some 'actual landscape,' from 'reality'?"[32] Lewis concludes, "Not only is western authorship suddenly exposed as contested, nervous, and disarmingly ambitious, but a new history of western literature begins to emerge."[33] Applying Lewis's questions to Royce and her narrative leads us to ask: What happens when we view Royce's narrative as a work of literature that imaginatively plays with and employs the strategies inherent in the western genre? And, consequently, what happens when we view Royce herself as a writer who uses these strategies for a specific rhetorical purpose? A "new history of western literature" emerges in Royce's document when we perceive her as a writer and her narrative as a literary creation.

Much critical work is yet to be done on authors like Sarah Royce. Exploring the use of authenticity as a rhetorical strategy in western women's narratives helps us to understand how the women attempted to validate their experiences, their narratives, and themselves as authors. When we begin to look at Royce's narrative as a constructed text rather than an "authentic" portrayal of life in Gold Rush California and consider Royce's role as author of the text, we not only challenge assumptions about authenticity, we also begin to see how Royce participated in the mythologizing of her own story and, as a result, the western woman's experience. Lewis claims that writers used three primary strategies to claim authenticity for their text: "through the memory of firsthand experience, through the notes and letters they wrote on the spot, and through reference to other recognized authorities."[34] Royce uses two of these three strategies: recounting her "memory of firsthand experience" and quoting from the diary kept on the trail. Her direct claim to primacy as one of the original settlers links her to the foundations of California's history as a state and underscores her own authority. Her use of the trope of authenticity lends credence to her story and supports her own role as the narrator of that story.

Royce documents her role as an eyewitness in two ways: first, by placing herself in the text as an observer of the western environment, a role that puts her in an intermediary position between the western setting and her readers, and second, in her repeated characterization of herself in California as an "old-timer." In the early sections of her narrative, Royce uses her position as an observer to portray a world on the margins, a kind of liminal space within which anything is possible. Once she settles into her new home in California, she takes on the persona of a seasoned inhabitant. The reflective quality of her work—looking back as she is, more than thirty years later, at earlier events—allows her to position herself convincingly as an authority on early California.

An Observer on the Threshold of the West

In Royce's writing, the western landscape that she is passing through presents itself as a threshold to another world. Quite literally, this other world that she seeks is the California known only to her traveling self as the place where she will find her "home nest." In another, more fanciful, sense the western landscape becomes an enchanted space: a bush can ignite as if by magic, people can expire quickly and decisively from the elements, and Royce herself can become a wanderer in a "far off, old-time desert" (43). Anthropologist Victor Turner's work has explored the three phases of transitional rites known as separation, margin or limen, and reaggregation. He defines the middle, liminal, state as one that is "neither here nor there, betwixt and between all fixed points of classification."[35] This is the transitional state that Royce encounters on the trail. In the context of the trail, she situates herself as the interpreter and mediator between her audience and the landscape.[36] As she herself navigates this margin, she experiences both external and internal transition.

As the Royces cross the desert—a critical juncture in their journey—they lose their way and are forced to seek out help and then turn back. This experience places Royce quite literally in the text as a filter for her readers' perception. Lost in the desert, Royce characterizes her search for help through the "gaze" with which she scrutinizes her surroundings and her situation: "With unwearied gaze my eyes swept, again and again, the shimmering horizon. There was no help or hope there" (38). Royce's gaze, fixed on the horizon, searching for help, suggests that she understands the thin protection her small party—including her husband—provides for her and her daughter. Royce writes: "Then I looked at what lay nearest. How short-lived our few remaining resources would be, unless fresh strength came soon from somewhere. How still it was. Only the sound of a few feeble breaths. It would not take many hours of starvation to quiet them forever. All the human aid we had could do but little now, and if, in trying to do that little, one more mistake were made, it must be fatal" (38).

As her gaze shifts from the distant prospect to those close at hand, Royce records the impending peril wrought by the party's mistakes. Characteristically, Royce invokes her religious faith in the face of what she perceives to be grave danger. But neither her belief nor the "calm strength" that she claims to derive from it can prepare her for or assuage the frustration of being forced to retrace their steps:

Turn back! What a chill the words sent through one. Turn back, on a journey like that; in which every mile had been gained by most earnest labor, growing more and more intense, until, of late, it had seemed that the certainty of advance with every step, was all that made the next step possible. And now for miles we were to *go back*. In all that long journey no steps ever seemed

so heavy, so hard to take, as those with which I turned my back
to the sun that afternoon of October 4ᵗʰ 1849. (39)

Royce's choice of words is interesting here as she repeatedly and
rhythmically focuses on the backward momentum of each step,
places herself as the one turning back in the last sentence ("*I*
turned *my* back"; emphasis added), and concludes with the date
of occurrence as if to time-stamp her experience for posterity.

   Despite her frustrations, she uses these experiences to position
herself as an authority. As she is wandering around, lost in the desert, she claims that the experience is one that only someone with
firsthand knowledge can truly comprehend: "Only a woman who
has been alone upon a desert with her helpless child can have any
adequate idea of my experience for the next hour or two" (39). A
few pages later, Royce again uses her experience to cast herself as
the eyewitness. She is observing the smoking remains of fires left
by "campers or Indians," when, in an instant, a small fire ignites
and almost as suddenly goes out right in front of her. She writes:
"It was a small incident, easily accounted for, but to my then over-
wrought fancy it made more vivid the illusion of being a wanderer
in a far off, old-time desert, and myself witnessing a wonderful
phenomenon" (43). The fire is presented to Royce, the eyewitness
observer, who then presents it to her readers as evidence that she
is, in fact, privy to an extraordinary spectacle. Royce as wanderer
in the "far off, old-time desert" inhabits a kind of liminal space
that, in her fancy, can exist simultaneously in this world that is
"easily accounted for" and in another far more exotic one.

   Earlier in her text, Royce inserts an odd, almost touristic
moment into her account that is notable because it is so different from the rest of her text, describing as it does a joyful burst
of energy in a story characterized more by plodding than exu-
berance, and notable too because it also positions her as an eyewitness. When the Royces reach Independence Rock on July 26,
Sarah Royce determines that she will climb it. She writes:

   I had long before determined to ascend it, if I ever reached it,
   and found it not too rash an undertaking. Another woman
   of our company joined me. One or two of her boys climbed

with us, and (just that she might have it to remember, and tell of) I took my little Mary. Of course I had to lift her from one projection to another most of the way; but we went leisurely, and her delight on reaching the top, our short rest there, and the view we enjoyed, fully paid for the labor. (24)

It is at this moment in the text that Royce's narrative threatens, however briefly, to turn into a travel narrative. This instance—and an accompanying one in California in which Royce depicts her excitement at seeing Sutter's Fort for the first time—is notable because it is uncharacteristic of her larger story and because it operates in several ways to authenticate her story. It places her in a real place on a specific date, and it casts the climbing of the rock as an important event—consequential enough for her to bring along her young daughter just so that she could say she had been there. It also allows Royce to depict herself as both a tourist and a guide shepherding others in their ascent. In most of her narrative, Royce portrays herself as following, but in this instance she takes the lead. Even as other travelers have inscribed their names on this famous halfway marker, Royce claims mastery of the landmark as, in her ascent and the subsequent account of the experience, she emphasizes the primacy of personal experience.[37]

If Royce's role is not always fixed, neither are the shifting environments she encounters. It is this very instability in the western environment that generates the greatest tension in her narrative. The blurring of interior and exterior space threatens the domestic sphere as the solid walls of home recede to be replaced with only a thin canvas-walled construction. The fact that canvas walls were common both in the wagons on the trail and in California offers little comfort to Royce. This blurring of spaces threatens Royce's attempts to construct a domestic (and therefore safe) space for herself and her family. The fluidity of space between the interior and the exterior endangers the very fabric of mid-nineteenth-century concepts of home that would almost certainly have informed Royce's thinking about the domestic sphere. Amy Kaplan writes that "Domesticity dominated middle-class women's writing and culture from the 1830s through the 1850s, a time when national boundaries were in violent flux."[38] Kaplan claims that what she calls "imperial domesticity" "continually projects a map of unregenerate outlying foreign terrain that both gives coherence to its boundaries and justifies its domesticating mission."[39] The creation of foreignness as that area outside of the domestic space reveals the need to create boundaries to protect the home-space and also underscores the potential threat when the domestic space cannot be clearly and cleanly defined.

For Royce, the domestic—on the trail and in the mining camps—becomes a liminal space where the outdoors threatens to encroach upon the interior of her various homes in disconcerting ways. At the beginning of her journey, Royce describes the anxiety she felt at the lack of shelter on the overland trail:

> Night was coming on. No house was within sight. Why did I look for one? I knew we were to camp; but surely there would be a few trees or a sheltering hillside against which to place our wagon. No; only the level prairies stretched on each side of the way. Nothing indicated a place for us,—a cozy nook, in which for the night we might be guarded, at least by banks of boughs. I had for months anticipated this hour, yet, not till it came did I realize the black dreariness of seeing night come on without house or home to shelter us and our baby girl. And this was to be the same for many weeks, perhaps months. It was a chilling prospect, and there was a terrible shrinking from it in my heart. (2)

Royce's "terrible shrinking" mirrors her own desire for retreat into a protected space that she will not find. The imagery she uses to describe this jarring disjuncture portrays a violently malicious nature calmed by the hand of the creator: "Thunder, lightning and wind seemed combined to tear our frail tenements to pieces; but the same Almighty Power that send the tempest, tempered it to us defenseless ones; and though the rain drove into our wagons, our food and clothing were not seriously injured" (15). Royce characterizes the storm as a malevolent force that threatens to encroach upon their interior spaces, thus calling into question the possibility of interiority in their compromised situation.

The lack of clearly defined interior and exterior space means for Royce that death itself cannot be screened away from the living, a point which is made apparent as she describes how her family must sleep amidst the storm with the body of a cholera victim just a few feet away: "The body of the dead man lay stretched upon a rudely constructed bier beside our wagon a few rods off, the sheet that was stretched over it flapped in the wind with a sound that suggested the idea of some vindictive creature struggling restlessly in bonds; while its white flutterings, dimly seen, confirmed the ghastly fancy" (14). In the waving of the fabric—meant to separate the man's body from open viewing—by the "vindictive" wind, Royce offers her readers a kind of "western gothic" in which the taint of death encroaches upon the living. With only the wagon as shelter, the Royces have little protection from this western *memento mori*.

The fears that were awakened upon the trail—of loss, abandonment, and homelessness—continue into her description of life in California. Royce depicts conditions in the mining camps as only slightly better than those she experienced on the trail. She writes of her reawakened anxiety:

> The sense of safety that came from having arrived where there was no danger of attacks from Indians, or of perishing of want or of cold on the desert, or in the mountains, was first so restful that I was willing, for awhile, to throw off anxiety; and, like a child fixing a play-house I sang as I arranged our few comforts in our tent. . . . Still, there was a lurking feeling of want of security from having only a cloth wall between us and out of doors. (60)

Her gravest concern in the mining camps comes not from exposure to the elements but from the threat of the intrusion of strangers upon her flimsy home (60). Because the division between interior and exterior are blurred by her exposed position in a canvas tent, strangers might transgress the normal boundaries that the walls of a framed house provide. In Royce's account, this threat is more imagined than real. Royce describes meeting two strangers when she was alone one day, one of whom had "one of the most

ferociously savage looking faces [she] ever saw" (104). Her fear
that they will return to her campsite at night keeps her on guard
all night. When she hears the sound of footsteps, she fears for her
life: "The sound came nearer. In a moment I should see somebody
come in sight. The step ceased; then the form of a man moved
cautiously out from the shadow of the bushes and turned from the
road towards the house. I scarcely breathed" (106). Royce fears
for the safety of herself and her family with the possible encroach-
ment of the interloper on her flimsy shelter. She later learns that
the stranger creeping around her tent was actually a friend; however, this fearful night convinces her to move closer to the mining
village for protection.

The social world Royce encounters in California is also a
liminal space where rules for behavior are not fixed. The transition from the fixed social space of the East, which held familiar
expectations for a middle-class woman like Royce, to one where
the basis for relationships and even identity are more fluid begins
when Royce sets out on the trail. As Deborah Lawrence writes, "As
she crossed its [the wilderness's] threshold, she began to slip out of
social relationships and familiar spaces that formed her stable, eastern identity."[40] Upon arriving in California, Royce notes that the
inhabitants seem particularly willing to transgress social boundaries out of convenience and opportunity. She gives several examples
of these transgressions, notably one in which a man attempts to
bring his mistress to a "Benevolent Society" ball. In this case, when
the man and his mistress are asked to leave, the rules for social
interaction are being defined as they are being imposed. What had
likely prompted him to bring her in the first place, however, is
the expectation and resulting misunderstanding that society is still
fluid enough to accept such unconventional arrangements. Royce
writes, "It was reported that he had previously boasted that he
could introduce 'Irene' anywhere in San Francisco; but the events
of that evening proved to him, as well as to others, that while
Christian women would forego ease and endure much labor in
order to benefit any who suffered, they would not welcome into
friendly association any who trampled upon institutions which lie
at the foundation of morality and civilization" (87–88). As Royce
seeks to solidify such social boundaries, it is characteristic that

in earlier experiences in the mining camps she rebuffed attempts to draw her into the social life of the camp by turning down a ball invitation, claiming to be "no dancer, and entirely unfitted to adorn any such scene" (63).

The transience that characterized Sarah Royce's early years in California and that thwarted her initial attempts to create a safe and secure home ended only when the family moved several years later to Grass Valley, where they remained for twelve years. As Royce indicates in her narrative, the transience that marked her young married life was hazardous to her highly valued domestic security and comfort. However, her experience simultaneously gives her the ability to speak as an authority. In her overland journey and her early years in California, Royce experiences a series of thresholds both real and imagined: first on the trail, which is itself a passage to another place and is characterized by forward movement (thwarted briefly by the party's backtracking), then, in California, both the physical experience of what Royce deems substandard housing and the social liminality of a place that is just beginning to consider and apply appropriate manners and mores. The California that Royce first encounters is a place on the threshold of statehood, and Royce's eyewitness observation of its admittance to the union, discussed in the next section, secures her place as an early Californian. Looking back, surveying this time period from the vantage point of security, Royce is still able to capture for her readers the insecurity of the new world she first encountered thirty years before.

The "Early Pioneer" Stakes Her Claim

I understand there is a gentleman in San Francisco, deeply interested in California history, who holds it to be a serious indication of spurious pretenses, if any one claiming to be an early Pioneer does not, within five minutes after beginning to talk about those old times, say that he has "seen the time when the tide water came up to Montgomery St." I hasten, therefore, to say that "I saw tide water come up to Montgomery St.," and, more, that it was on one occasion with difficulty I avoided stepping into it, within a very short distance of the door of our Hotel. (77)

In the anecdote above, we can see Royce staking her own claim as an early pioneer. Royce not only aligns herself with the early Gold Rush settlers, she does the other long-time inhabitants one better by depicting herself as almost stepping into the floodwaters that validate their authority. Once in California, the quotations from her trail diary cease. As she settles into life in California, Royce's voice and tone become reflective, establishing her position among the foundational citizens of early California. Rather than setting Royce apart from other Gold Rush narratives written by women, the strategies Royce uses to emphasize her authority are characteristic of the genre of pioneer reminiscences. David Wrobel writes: "The old pioneer reminiscers of a century ago . . . did not just remember the hardships of their westward journeys and play up the object lessons that younger generations could learn from their trials on the trails; they also emphasized the fact that they had been 'in place' for longer than other white residents."[41] This emphasis on longevity is an attempt to give their perspectives on events credibility.

Royce's purpose in her narrative becomes clear when her work is compared with that of another female '49er, Luzena Stanley Wilson. The outline of these women's experiences is strikingly similar, which makes the different ways they negotiate their environment all the more telling. The Royces and the Wilsons took the same overland route, with the Royces just five weeks behind the Wilson party.[42] Both women were caught up in the same flood that engulfed Sacramento in January 1850,[43] and both received similar treatment by the locals, who offered each woman a portion of a room cordoned off by sheets as a place of refuge from the rising waters.

There are also notable similarities in the way the women depict their experiences. Both begin their stories at the jumping-off point—Wilson in Missouri and Royce in Iowa.[44] Both women face hardship and death along the trail and portray the harder aspects in a kind of frontier gothic tone. Wilson recounts the first time she witnessed the death of a fellow traveler:

Everything was at first weird and strange in those days, but custom made us regard the most unnatural events as usual. I remember even yet with a shiver the first time I saw a man buried without the formality of a funeral and the ceremony of coffining. We were sitting by the camp fire, eating breakfast, when I saw two men digging and watched them with interest, never dreaming their melancholy object until I saw them bear from their tent the body of their comrade, wrapped in a soiled gray blanket, and lay it on the ground. Ten minutes later the soil was filled in, and in a short half hour the caravan moved on, leaving the lonely stranger asleep in the silent wilderness, with only the winds, the owls, and coyotes to chant a dirge.[45]

Using remarkably similar language, Royce recounts a scene of death made all the more frightening by the mournful soundtrack of the Indians who followed them:

Not many yards beyond [the body of the deceased man], a party of Indians, who had, for a day or two, been playing the part of friendly hangers on to one of the large companies, had raised a rude skin tent, and built a fire, round which they were seated on the ground, looking unearthly in its flickering light and chanting, hour after hour, a wild melancholy chant, varied by occasional high, shrill notes as of distressful appeal. The minor key ran through it all. I knew it was a death dirge.[46]

Royce's account is characteristically the longer and more descriptive of the two, but notable similarities—their proximity to the dead body, the "voice" of the wind, the melancholy atmosphere, and the dirge as background music for the scene—suggest that these elements had become or were becoming an assumed part of the telling of the western story.

Underlying both women's stories is their claim to authority. Like Royce, Wilson asserts that the westward journey can only be comprehended through firsthand knowledge: "Nothing but actual experience will give one an idea of the plodding, unvarying monotony, the vexations, the exhaustive energy, the throbs of hope, the depths of despair, through which we lived."[47] Wilson also recognizes the lack of protection afforded by flimsy shelter during the Sacramento flood of 1850 when she claims that "The canvas roof seemed like a sieve, and water dropped on us from every crevice."[48] Unlike Royce, Wilson portrays herself as one who is comfortable in the liminal spaces of the western environment. When the Wilson family finally does secure a framed house, unlike Royce, she even finds the experience confining: "I had grown so accustomed to sleeping in the open air, that the first night we slept under a roof I absolutely suffered from a sense of suffocation, although there were neither doors nor windows to the structure."[49] Wilson's adaptability allows her to look at her experiences as a kind of adventure. Finding it easier than Royce does to operate within uncertain environments, she accepts an invitation to a ball from Spanish neighbors, which was, she claims, "prompted quite as much by curiosity as by my friendly feelings for my neighbors."[50] The divisions between herself and the people she encounters that characterize Royce's portrayal of California society are transgressed in Wilson's account as Wilson decisively crosses boundaries.

The differences between the two women's accounts extend to their views of progress and development in California as they establish their own vantage point of early settlerhood. At the end of their narratives, both women review the changes wrought in California during their tenancy and claim the role of early settler. Wilson focuses on such diverse changes as advances in farming and animal husbandry, the behavior of children, and the taming of social practices and entertainment. In the changes in California that Wilson laments, fallow land is cultivated, pigs and chickens no longer root and scratch with impunity, well-dressed children go to school instead of out to play with the pigs and chickens, and the raucous amusements of times past have been tamed by the coming of better judgment and big-city sensibility. Wilson writes:

The old-time Sabbath amusements of riding bucking mustangs into the saloons, drinking all day at the various bars, running foot-races, playing poker, and finishing the day with a free fight are things of the past. The sobering influence of civilization has removed all such exciting but dangerous pastimes as playing scientific games of billiards by firing at the balls with a pistol, taking off the heads of the decanters behind the counter with a quick shot, and making the bar-keeper shiver for his well-curled hair.[51]

Socially, Wilson sees the arrival of city folk as stultifying to the dances til dawn of times past. She sees the changes and laments them as she writes, "With the stages went the rollicking, unassuming fun of the country, and with the railroads came in the aping of city airs and the following of city fashions."[52] Literally, each form of transportation brings in a different sort of people. She concludes her narrative with the concern that all of her contemporaries are dying off, and soon nothing will be left of these early times: "Day by day the circle narrows, and in a few more years there will be none of us left to talk over the 'early days.'"[53] The last words of her story emphasize loss as she considers how life has moved away from the familiar past.

Similarly, Royce enumerates events that place her at the scene of early California history. Unlike Wilson, however, she portrays most of these occurrences as positive developments in a linear timeline of progress. She writes: "We saw the beginnings of that system of 'street grading' which has since so transformed the face of the site of San Francisco. We gazed with terror on the awful fire of May 4th 1850. We witnessed the erection of new churches, and the inauguration of religious newspapers" (82). Notable also was the admission of California into the union—an event that she witnessed firsthand as she watched a steamer enter the port "displaying the words 'California Admitted!'" (83). She describes the jubilation of the people as they exclaimed, "'Now we are at home again!'" (83). She talks with a sense of nostalgia for the business ventures that "still live, for good or ill, in the lives of hundreds of Californians" (83). And she counters the old saying that "All the old Pioneers are poor men" with her assertion that "Quite a number of those Pioneers laid the foundation even in those early days of extravagant undertakings, for permanent business, and substantial prosperity" (83–84). These men, she claims, "are now among the pillars of California society; with well educated families grown up about them, who, in their turn, are rearing children to follow in the good paths of their grand-sires" (84). One can almost hear Royce arguing for her own role as one of the "pillars of California society." Royce recognizes that the saying does have a basis in fact as she wittily recounts: "Here and there was an individual in whom all the conditions just named [inexperience and an inflated sense of ability], met, and that man was bound to make a desperate dash, and as surely bound to fail, and, alas, almost certainly bound to repeat the same experience every three or five years since, till, 'the old Californian *is* a poor man'" (84). As a place rife with speculation and other moral pitfalls, early California, as Royce describes it, is a potential breeding ground for greed and destitution. The current prosperity that Royce depicts in the 1880s is a result of those good citizens who did not fall prey to this moral decay.

Royce takes the bad with the good, and at the conclusion of her narrative she once again references the great events of the previous thirty years, among them "the Washoe fever that sent thousands surging wildly over the high ridges they had once dreaded to approach," "the awful roar of Civil War [which] burst from cannons on the Atlantic Shore and rolled over every mountain and plain till it met the moaning surges of the Pacific," and the overland railroad that "helped to carry prosperity to California" (109). Referring to the "first adopted children" of the state and ostensibly counting herself among their number, Royce specifically names both the impulse of the historian to understand the early years of the state and the desire of the settlers to inscribe their own memories: "Those remaining have grown old, and look back on years of wonderful experiences which they sometimes wish could be recorded along with the history of their adopted State; for their children and their children's children to read, that they might learn to love and reverence the God who through all the devious paths of life ever guides safely those who trust and obey Him" (110). In this simple statement, Royce gives her readers an understanding of her own impulse to write and claims the authority to do so.

In a final story, which Royce signals is her conclusion, she returned to the home in San Francisco where she lived thirty-four years earlier. She talked with the owner of the house about "those old times" and then "ascended to the high veranda and stood upon the very spot where in October 1850 I had stood with another old Californian, and seen the Oregon coming into port with 'California Admitted' streaming at her mast head" (110). She writes that as she stood upon the veranda, she was over-come by the experience and is, for once, unable to characterize it for her readers: "Words are powerless to express the thoughts and emotions of one permitted, like myself at that moment, to step backward in time thirty four years" (110). Royce comes full circle, and it is in the circularity of her journey that she ends her narrative: "In a country proverbial for the instability of all things, it is rare for persons and places, entirely separated for a genera-tion of time, thus to come together again" (110). Unlike Wilson, who concludes her narrative with a sense of loss and lament for times past, Royce depicts the closing of a loop. In her pairing of the historian and the eyewitness in the earlier quote, both of whom are recording the foundations of the state, Royce suggests that there are two stories to tell and that the history is not com-plete without the personal account. The story that the children and the children's children will know must be one, for Royce, that includes her own voice.

Four years after the conclusion of Royce's narrative, Josiah Sr. died of a stroke on June 23, 1888 in Los Gatos, and Sarah moved to San Jose to live with her daughter Ruth, who by then was the first librarian at San Jose State University, known at the time as California State Normal School. She continued to participate in church activities and taught a Sunday School class for boys during her years in San Jose.[54] In his biography of Josiah Jr., Robert V. Hine relates an incident from April 1891 where Sarah was struck in the head by a heavyset man who inadvertently bumped into her in the San Jose post office. The large gash that she suffered from the accident seems to have set her on a downward spiral of illness that weakened her constitution and left her lethargic and short of breath. Nearly seven months after the accident, on November 24, 1891, Sarah Royce died. She left behind her four surviving children and a manuscript of her story that would come to be considered one of the finest first-person accounts of the Gold Rush from a woman's perspective.

When Sarah Royce set down her pen at the conclusion of her narrative in 1886, she had no way of knowing that her story would eventually be published and read widely by students, scholars, and western history enthusiasts. Although she intentionally shapes herself in her narrative in the image of the iconic pioneer woman, Royce could not have known that her words would play a public role in representing the western woman. She did not know that she would be the subject of a children's textbook or that she would be portrayed in Chautauqua performances.[55] She especially had no way to know that pages from her handwritten manuscript would appear on a Website on the Internet.[56] It is questionable whether the woman who retreated from society as "being no dancer" would approve.

Sarah Royce has become an important figure in western studies because she offers us a glimpse into a bygone world. However, the importance of Royce's story extends far beyond its role as an historical artifact. David Wrobel writes, "the true significance of the frontier in American history may lie less in any role the frontier actually played in shaping a national character and institutions than in the powerful selective memories of the frontier's influence."[57] I hope that in perusing this volume you will see that Royce's importance lies in what her story tells us about the construction of narrative and the role of authenticity and authorship for a woman who is writing alongside the historians of her day as she also attempts to characterize an experience that has become the stuff of western myth.

A Note on the Text

Sarah Royce's original manuscript is held in the Bancroft Library at the University of California, Berkeley. It is a handwritten document composed of 107 numbered pages. In keeping with modern practices for scholarly editing, I have presented Royce's narrative as close to the original handwritten manuscript as I could while still maintaining the readability of the document. I have kept much of Royce's punctuation and paragraphing. Royce rarely uses new paragraphs and never uses section or chapter breaks. Paragraph returns are indicated in her manuscript either, conventionally, by a new line of text or by a space in the middle of a line. I have maintained much of her original paragraphing, using additional paragraph returns only when they were necessary to enhance the readability of the document. I have restored five sections of her narrative excised from the previous publication of her text. These excised sections range in length from several lines to several pages. In two instances these excisions, which include her final story, offer claims to authenticity and authorship that are crucial to our understanding of Sarah Royce the writer.

In one instance, three and a half pages have been removed from the original manuscript. An accompanying note on the back of page 93 of her manuscript reads: "The remainder of page 93, also pages 94, 95, & 96 are cut out of this manuscript." Directly below this note, written in a different hand, is an identifying note that claims: "The above is the hand writing of Ruth Royce, youngest daughter of Sarah Eleanor Royce." It is signed "M. J. Compton." The contents of the pages excised from the manuscript are a mystery. I have included a note within the text indicating the place where the material has been removed. I have included my own content notes to her document.

Although her document covers much more than just the period of the overland journey, I have also restored her original title—*Across the Plains*—as it is the title Royce, herself, gave to the work and a phrase she uses twice within her narrative. In reviewing bibliographic citations of western narratives, I have found the title *Across the Plains* to be conventional to this genre (many of these texts include this phrase in the title). This suggests that the westward trek was a pivotal, life-altering moment that resonated with these pioneers even years after the experience, shaping not only their own stories but also how they defined themselves to the world.

ACROSS THE PLAINS

On the last day of April, 1849 we began our journey to California. Our outfit consisted of a covered wagon, well loaded with provisions, and such preparations for sleeping, cooking etc., as we had been able to furnish, guided only by the light of "Fremont's Travels," and the suggestions, often conflicting, of the many who, like ourselves, utter strangers to camping life, were setting out for the "Golden Gate." Our wagon was drawn by three yoke of oxen and one yoke of cows. The latter being used in the teams only part of the time. Their milk was of course to be a valuable part of our subsistence. Nearly a year before we had bidden farewell to all our friends in the East, and we had been living for several months in a pleasant village in Iowa [Tipton], about twenty miles from the Mississippi.[1] So we had nearly the whole state of Iowa to cross as merely introductory to the journey proper to California. Council Bluffs was the point for which we were to aim first, and that was to be the place of starting upon the grand pilgrimage. The morning of that 30th of April was not very bright; but neither was it very gloomy. Rain might come within an hour, but then the sun might come out,—I would not consent to delay our departure for fear of the weather. Had I not made up my mind to encounter many storms? If we were going, let us go, and meet what we were to meet bravely.

So I seated myself in the wagon, my little two-year-old Mary was placed beside me, my husband and the other man of our little company started the team, and we were on our way. The day turned out by no means unpleasant. Our first noon lunch was eaten by the whole party, seated in the front part of the wagon, while the cattle, detached from the wagon but not unyoked, grazed near by. After a short rest we again moved on. The afternoon wore quietly away, the weather being rather brighter and warmer than in the morning. And now night was coming on. No house was within sight. Why did I look for one? I knew we were to camp; but surely there would be a few trees or a sheltering hillside against which to place our wagon. No; only the level prairie stretched on each side of the way. Nothing indicated a place for us,—a cozy nook, in which for the night we might be guarded, at least by banks and boughs.

I had for months anticipated this hour, yet, not till it came did I realize the blank dreariness of seeing night come on without house or home to shelter us and our baby-girl. And this was to be the same for many weeks, perhaps months. It was a chilling prospect, and there was a terrible shrinking from it in my heart; but I kept it all to myself and we were soon busy making things as comfortable as we could for the night. Our wagon was large, we were provided with straw and plenty of bedclothes; and soon a very tolerable resting place was ready for us. Our little Mary had been happy as a lark all day, and now sank to sleep in her straw and blanket bed, as serenely as though she were in a palace, on a downy pillow!

At first the oppressive sense of homelessness, and an instinct of watchfulness, kept me awake. Perhaps it was not to be wondered at in one whose life so far had been spent in city or town surrounded by the accompaniments of civilization and who was now, for the first time in her life, "camping out." However, quiet sleep came at last; and in the morning, there was a mildly exultant feeling which comes from having kept silent through a cowardly fit, and finding the fit gone off.

But the oxen and cows were found to be "gone off" too, and my first entry in my "Pilgrim's Diary" was made at very unwelcome leisure "staying by the stuff" with my little one, while the men were recovering the animals. It was late in the forenoon when they were brought and yoked up, and our second day's journey was begun. It soon became plain that the hard facts of this pilgrimage would require patience, energy, and courage fully equal to what I had anticipated when I had tried to stretch my imagination to the utmost. These facts came first in such mean, vexing forms. Deep mud-holes in which the wagon would stick fast; or, still worse, sloughs,—called by the western people "sloos,"—covered with turf that appeared perfectly sound, but which would break when the full weight came upon it, and let the wheels in nearly to the hubs; closing round the spokes so tightly that digging, alone, would free them. In these cases, the whole, or nearly the whole, of the contents of the wagon had to be unloaded, often in very miry places sometimes in the rain, while the men had to "put shoulder to the wheels" and lift them out by main force. Several times while we were all busy in such a scene, the cattle wandered off into a wood or over a hill and hours would be lost in getting them together. Oftener they were lost in the morning, for they must be turned out to graze during the night, and then the best traveling part of the day would be gone, before we could move on. This happened on our fourth day out.

Looking into my old diary, which I kept in those days, though in a very broken, desultory manner, I find the following entry, for May 3rd 1849. "The sloughs were very bad, stopping us repeatedly during the day; and just at dusk we found ourselves fast, in a most dreary swamp. We had encountered in the middle of the afternoon a tremendous blow and rain while out on the open prairie;—the night looked threatening, and before morning we were visited by a heavy thunder storm. The next day,—Friday,—was so inclement as to prevent traveling. I cooked as well as I could by a log fire in a strong north-east blow. My little Mary, to my great surprise, was cheerful and happy, playing in the wagon, with various simple things I provided for her, singing and laughing most of the time. Saturday morning, though the weather still continued cloudy, we attempted to proceed, but the rain had softened the ground so much that we found ourselves 'stuck' almost every half mile. After a hard day's work we succeeded in reaching the little town of Tipton, only 3 miles from where we started in the morning. Here we spent our first Sabbath out; the clouds still threatening and the rain falling every few minutes."

At this point we met with three other wagons, and three days after, at Cedar River, with several others, all bound for California.

There was certainly satisfaction in having company for we could, by uniting teams, help each other over hard places, saving much time. But the weather still continued unfavorable, and I find recorded for Friday May 11th, which was the day after crossing the Cedar River, that "we had a hard day's drive through a drenching rain, arriving at Iowa City toward night." Here we spent our second Sunday, and on Monday morning crossed the Iowa River which I see I noted as "A pretty stream, reminding me of *my own, old Genesee*; especially when I saw one, solitary steamboat lying at the landing some distance from the City."[2]

Storms, bad roads and swollen streams, continued to impede our way nearly every day till we reached Council Bluffs. Referring again to my journal, I find on the 20th of May we "were visited by a thunder storm," and, on the 21st "Were overtaken during the afternoon by two tremendous storms of thunder, lightning and wind. Encamped, just as the last one burst upon us, on the lee side of a beautiful grove; and, at the close of the storm, as the clouds broke, the most brilliant and perfect rain-bow I ever saw completely arched the lovely scene."

"May 22. Reached Indian Creek which was so swollen by the late rains as to be impassable. Had to remain there until the men built a bridge; which took them till the next day at noon; and after crossing the stream, our way for some distance lay through flat bottom-land, where in several places the water stood two feet deep."

When we reached Fort Des Moines we fell in with several more little companies from different points, nearly all of whom gave discouraging reports of their own progress, and of the news they were receiving, at this point, in various ways, from others who were on the way to California. From Council Bluffs, and other crossing places on the Missouri River, came word that Cholera was raging among the emigrants; with various other depressing stories about difficulties in obtaining proper supplies of wholesome provisions, such as could be carried on so long a journey. To this was added the assertion that such an immense number had already left the Missouri, and were far on their way, that the grass was all eaten up, and no more animals could live on the great plains. All this we heard, and all this we talked over, but still we

went on, and at the end of one month and four days after beginning our travels, we reached Council Bluffs.

Here we found a city of wagons, some of which had been there
many days waiting their turn to cross the great river. But we were
consoled by being assured that the ferry men were working as fast
as possible, and that probably in a week or so, all now camped
ready for crossing would be over the Missouri. Notwithstanding
the crowd of people, most of them strangers to each other; thrown
together in such new and inconvenient circumstances with much
to try patience; and all standing necessarily more or less in the
position of rivals for the local conveniences which campers so
soon learn to look for and prize; still the utmost quiet and good
humor mostly prevailed. The great majority of the crowd were
men, generally working men of ordinary intelligence, farmers and
mechanics, accustomed to the comforts and amenities of domestic
life, and most of them evidently intending to carry more or less of
these agreeable things with them "across the plains."

Occasionally these men were accompanied by wife and children, and their wagons were easily distinguished by the greater
number of conveniences, and house-hold articles they carried,
which here, in this time of prolonged camping, were often, many
of them, disposed about the outside of the wagon, in a home-like
way; and, where bushes, trees or logs formed partial enclosures, a
kitchen or sitting room quite easily suggested itself to a feminine
heart, yearning for home. The few women who caught glimpses of
each other, or, in some cases, were thrown nearer together, in this
motley gathering, were in general very kind to each other and to
each other's children. But, waiting as they were for the very first
chance to cross the Missouri, and expecting after that to travel
in different companies, there was no motive for any particular
mutual interest.

After patiently waiting some days for our turn to cross the
river, it came at last, and on Friday the 8th of June we ventured
ourselves and our little all, on board a very uncertain looking ferry-boat, and were slowly conveyed across the turbid and
unfriendly-looking Missouri. The cattle were "swum" across the
stream; the men driving them in and frightening them off from
the shore in various ways, until a few of the leaders reached the

flats on the opposite side. As soon as they were seen to come out of the water there, the others easily followed. A few of the many thus crossed were driven by the strong current beyond the flats and lost; but most of them crossed safely. From the place where we landed the ascent up the bluff was steep and dusty. Arriving at the top we were on an almost level plain, with only here and there a tree or two; though there was a body of timber a mile or two to the southwest. Not very far from the river we began to see the few scattered buildings of Trader's Point, the Indian Agency for this part of Nebraska Territory. So few and far between were the houses that I scarcely remember any thing but a blacksmith's shop and, not far from it, a pretty good-sized log house. Yet, on that spot Omaha City soon after grew to fair proportions, and has now for many years flourished. A slight accident had broken something about the wagon, and we stopped at the blacksmith shop to have it repaired. The other wagons passed on to the place of encampment for the night which was to be in the edge of the before mentioned timber.

Just as the blacksmith began work on our wagon, the gentlemanly Indian Agent, whom we had seen at Council Bluffs, came to us and kindly insisted upon my going with my little girl to his home, which proved to be the good-sized log house I had noticed, and resting there till my husband was ready to proceed. I gratefully accepted, and his hospitality did not cease until we had all three partaken of a bountiful supper prepared by his kind-hearted old negro cook, and had enjoyed a good rest and social chat beside his ample fire-place. He then helped us into our wagon, directed us to our camp grounds, two miles distant, expressed his good wishes for our long journey, and bade us good night. That was my farewell to the fag-end of civilization on the Atlantic side of the Continent. I saw no house from that time till we passed within view of the few dwellings at Fort Laramie; and did not again eat a meal in a house, until urged to do so once only by an hospitable Mormon woman, beside whose garden fence we had permission to locate our wagon, during our stay in Salt Lake City.

From our first arrival at Council Bluffs we had been annoyed by begging and pilfering Indians; male and female. To attempt to satisfy them was out of the question, for the most trifling thing bestowed on one would bring a dozen more. So our only defence was to keep them decidedly and quietly at a distance. Few of them could understand our words and we had to act with most emphatic dignity to keep them at all in proper place. On the western side of the Missouri they became more numerous, swarming about us at every pause in our way from the crossing of the ferry till night closed in but then they disappeared; and the Agent assured us that they were gone, not "to bed," but to their sleep among the bushes and sand hills; and that they would not dare to molest us so near the Agency; so, we might go, without fear, to camp. His words proved true, and we arrived safely at our place of stopping for the first night in an Indian Country. The next day was spent mostly by the men in organizing a regular company, with Captain, and subordinate officers whose duties and prerogatives were set forth in rules and by-laws then and there adopted. The few women in the company were busy meantime in cooking, washing, mending up clothes, etc. Notwithstanding the disheartening reports circulated among us for the past two weeks at different points in our way, hopefulness and unflinching resolution upon the whole prevailed. Some few there were, no doubt, who would have turned back; but they were involved either in family or business relations with others more resolute, or more rash; and, seeing the uselessness of resistance, they took up their part of the daily toil, in most cases, without complaining.

A number in the company tried to incorporate in the by-laws a rule that every Sunday should be a day of rest; but they only succeeded in gaining a general assent to camping on Sundays when the necessities and dangers of the way did not demand uninterrupted traveling. The majority insisted that the lateness of the season,—we being nearly the last emigrants to cross the Missouri,—and the importance of keeping near to larger companies just ahead, made it imperative that we should set out the very next morning; although it was Sunday.[3] Accordingly on the 10th of June we left our first campground west of the Missouri, and launched forth upon a journey in which, we all knew, from that hour there was not the least chance of turning back. The morning was bright and the scene animating. We were up early, breakfast was dispatched, and then came the bustle of packing our wagons, which was done by one man belonging to each wagon, while the other one, or two, yoked the cattle. In the few cases where there were women they were, without exception, seen doing their full share of the work. When all was ready the Captain gave the word of command, "Roll out!" and wagon after wagon fell into line in the order which had been assigned them.

For an hour or two we moved on with as lively a pace as oxen could well keep up. The sun shone brightly, and all looked hopeful. We were approaching rolling hills between which, we could see, our road lay. Suddenly, numerous dark moving objects appeared upon the hills in the distance, on both sides of the road. What could they be? Had some of the large companies ahead camped and turned out their cattle? Or, could it be, that we were about to have our first sight of a herd of buffalo? As we drew nearer they proved to be Indians, by hundreds; and soon they had ranged themselves along on each side of the way. A group of them came forward, and at the Captain's command our company halted, while he with several others went to meet the Indians and hold a parley. It turned out that they had gathered to demand the payment of a certain sum per head for every emigrant passing through this part of the country, which they claimed as their own. The men of our company after consultation, resolved that the demand was unreasonable; that the country we were traveling over belonged to the United States, and that these red men had no right to stop us. The Indians were then plainly informed that the company meant to proceed at once without paying a dollar. That if unmolested, they would not harm any thing; but if the Indians attempted to stop them, they would open fire with all their rifles and revolvers. At the Captain's word of command all the men of the company then armed themselves with every weapon to be found in their wagons. Revolvers, knives, hatchets, glittered in their belts; rifles and guns bristled on their shoulders. The drivers raised aloft their long whips, the rousing words "Go 'long Buck!"—"Bright!"—"Dan!" were given all along the line, and we were at once moving between long but not very compact rows of half naked red-skins; many of them well armed; others carrying but indifferent weapons; while all wore in their faces the expression of sullen disappointment, mingled with a half-defiant scowl, that suggested the thought of future night attacks, when darkness and thickets should give them greater advantage. For the present, however, they had evidently made up their minds to let us pass, and we soon lost sight of them.

But another enemy, unseen, and without one audible word of demand or threat, was in that very hour advancing upon us, and made our wagon his first point of attack. The oldest of the men who had joined company with my husband, complained of intense pain and sickness, and was soon obliged to lie down in the wagon, which, being large, gave room for quite a comfortable bed behind the seat where Mary and I sat. Soon, terrible spasms convulsed him; the Captain was called, examined the case, and ordered a halt. Medicine was administered which afforded some relief. About this time a horseman or two appeared, with the intelligence that some companies in advance of us were camped at the ford of the Elkhorn River, not more than two miles distant, and that there was a physician among them. We therefore made the sick man as comfortable as we could, and went on. Arrived at the encampment the Doctor pronounced the disease Asiatic Cholera. Everything was done that could be under the circumstances, but nothing availed, and in two or three hours the poor old man expired. The most prompt and energetic sympathy was shown by our fellow travelers. The fact was at once recognized that close contact with the disease for several hours, had exposed us to contagion, and had also made necessary the disinfecting of our wagon and all it contained. There were in the encampment those who had tents as well as wagons, and soon a comfortable tent, with a cot bed and other conveniences, was placed at our disposal till our things could be disinfected.

That Sunday night was one never to be forgotten by me. I positively refused to lie down, because there was room and covering for only one besides Mary; my husband had been on guard the night before and on most exhausting duty all day; so I insisted upon his resting, while I sat by my little one, leaning my head on her pillow, and tried to sleep. But a storm began in the evening. The wind moaned fitfully, and rain fell constantly. I could not sleep. I rose and walked softly to the tent door, put the curtains aside and looked out. The body of the dead man lay stretched upon a rudely constructed bier beside our wagon a few rods off, the sheet that was stretched over it flapped in the wind with a sound that suggested the idea of some vindictive creature struggling restlessly in bonds; while its white flutterings, dimly seen, confirmed the ghastly fancy. Not many yards beyond, a party of Indians,—who had, for a day or two, been playing the part of friendly hangers-on to one of the large companies,—had raised a rude skin tent, and built a fire, round which they were seated on the ground, looking unearthly in its flickering light, and chanting, hour after hour, a wild melancholy chant, varied by occasional high, shrill notes as of distressful appeal. The minor key ran through it all. I knew it was a death dirge.

Morning came at last. In the early dawn the body of the old man was laid in the grave that had been dug in a hillside nearby. Then came the work of cleansing the wagon, washing bed-clothes and thoroughly sunning and airing everything; for the storm was over and the sun shone very warmly. Before we had half done this work, the crossing of the Elkhorn was begun by the other companies. The wagons and people crossed on rafts and the cattle were "swum." By one or two o'clock p.m. we were all across and we finished our drying and airing on the west side. Soon after leaving the Elkhorn we struck the Platt River and now felt ourselves fairly launched out "on the plains." The next Wednesday morning, June 13th, before dawn we were visited by one of the most terrible storms I ever recollect witnessing. Thunder, lightning and wind seemed combined to tear our frail tenements to pieces; but the same Almighty Power that sent the tempest, tempered it to us defenseless ones; and though the rain drove into our wagons, our food and clothing were not seriously injured.

The next morning, just three days from the time old Mr. R——. had been buried, the first news that met our ears was that two more of our company were ill with the same fatal disease. Before the first watch of that night was set, one of them was laid in his lonely grave. I here quote again from my diary, which I "wrote up" a few days after these events. "Now indeed a heavy gloom hung round us. The destroyer seemed let loose upon our camp. Who would go next? What if my husband should be taken and leave us alone in the wilderness? What if I should be taken and leave my little Mary motherless? Or, still more distracting thoughts, what if we both should be laid low, and she be left a destitute orphan, among strangers, in a land of savages? Such thoughts would rush into my mind, and for some hours these gloomy forebodings heavily oppressed me; but I poured out my heart to God in prayer, and He gave me comfort and rest. I felt a full assurance that He would not afflict beyond our strength to bear. I committed my precious child into His hands entirely, claiming for her His promises, and His guardianship. I said from my heart 'Thy will be done.' Then peace took possession of my soul, and, spite of threatening ills, I felt strong for duty and endurance."

The second of the two sick men soon began to show favorable symptoms and in a few days recovered. From that time we had no more cases of cholera among our fellow travelers; though we passed a number of graves of its victims, and heard of deaths in other companies who camped not far from us.

On Saturday evening June 16th we arrived at the crossing of the Loup Fork of the Platt River. Here we found two companies, who had been camped there some days waiting for the waters to go down so that they could find a fording place. The bed of the Loup is, for miles, formed of quick-sand, so that where teams crossed in safety one day there might be deep holes the next. Especially after the waters had been swollen by heavy rains, as had lately been the case, it was impossible to be sure of a fording place without the most careful exploration, which of course involved considerable danger. A man had been drowned only a short time before our arrival, by venturing too hastily forward, when nearly across. He had found the water so shallow thus far, that he became too sanguine, and stepped suddenly into a deep channel, where the rushing water and sand soon swallowed him up. On the third day it was announced that the water had sufficiently subsided for us to attempt the passage; though there was still rather an ugly current near the farther shore. On our side there was shallow water for some rods through which our ordinary teams could pull a lightly-loaded wagon. Then there was an island of sand; and beyond that, the current was so deep and strong that teams would have to be doubled, and long ropes used. Moreover the greatest dispatch was necessary; for the sands shifted so constantly that the bottom changed more or less every hour.

As the quickest way of working, our teams were to take to the island two or three wagons at a time, then, fastening all the cattle to one wagon, with several men to drive, they were to rush that one rapidly across the deeper stream, and return for another. As fast as one standing-place on the island was vacated another wagon was driven over the shallow water to be ready for its turn; and thus one fresh team was used to each wagon at the hardest point. It was a little exciting for us women to take our seats, with our children beside us, and be drawn upon those treacherous sands we had heard so much of for two or three days; and it became startling when we felt the wagon trembling under us, as in a lively earthquake. The vibrations did not cease while we stood on the island, the wheels perpetually settling with short jerks into the sands; had we been obliged to stay there long we should have sunk to the hubs. But the men and faithful cattle worked nobly, and in due time we were west of the treacherous Loup Fork.

A few days after this we had a new and unexpected experience in the way of a stampede of cattle. On camping for the night each company of wagons always formed a corral by placing the wagons one before the other in such a position as to make a large circle. The tongue of each wagon dropped its end to the ground as the cattle were loosed from it, and the wagon in front was backed up so close as to leave barely room for a person to step in and out. A space, large enough to form a gateway, was left between the back of the first wagon and the front of the last, and into this gateway the cattle were driven at night, after they had well pastured; and the gateway was closed by ox-chains, securely fastened to the wheels of the two terminating wagons. Then a guard, of two or three men, was set, who patrolled on the outside of the corral, and were changed after midnight. On the night of the 19th of June our wagon was one of the terminating ones with its back to the gateway. On Wednesday morning June 20th I was awakened between three and four o'clock, by the sound of rain upon the wagon-top. It was quite a moderate shower, and I lay thinking, in a calm mood, when a flash of lightning came, followed in a moment by a strange rushing sound, which quickly became loud as thunder.

The wagon began to shake violently, then to move as if pushed sideways by a great force, then it was lifted and thrown violently over on its side; there was a crash of breaking wheels and chains, the rapid tramp of cattle became distinct for a minute, and then was lost in the distance. When we and our neighbors on the other side of the gateway, had picked ourselves up, and out, and found that none of us were much hurt, we began to try to account for the catastrophe, and examine its extent. The cattle must have been frightened by the flash of lightning. Those near the entrance of the corral instinctively tried to escape, others near pressed upon them, the panic grew, till, in their frantic struggles, they overturned the two chained wagons. At that moment the chains must have broken and cleared the passage-way, or they would have trampled us to death. There were some unimportant injuries done to both the wagons and to some of their contents; but the grand calamity was the breaking of three wheels; one of ours, and two of the other. We had, a day or two before, entered upon a stage of the journey marked in our guide-books as being destitute of timber for nearly two hundred miles, with the exception of one, solitary tree,— about midway of the distance—marked down as "The Lone Tree." Just as we had found out the worst of our breakage, the Captain of the company came near, and, after gazing a moment in speechless consternation, exclaimed, "Three wheels broke all to smash, and fifty miles from timber!"

It was true, and the fact was a hard one, and yet strange elasticity of mind, we laughed heartily at the grotesque speech. But now, what was to be done? In the first place, the cattle had "stampeded," and were all gone. How, and when could they be got back? Often in such cases they ran themselves to death. But even while we thus questioned, we were told that at the first alarm, some of the men had mounted the few horses owned in the company, and were last seen gaining upon the swiftest fugitives; while others, on foot, had already succeeded in turning back some of the more gentle ones. But those broken wheels, how could they be repaired in this desert? It soon turned out that there was a blacksmith in the company, with some tools, and a few odd pieces of hard wood; there were also two families who had brought with them wide, hard-wood boards, two or three feet long, which they used for tables while camping. These were freely contributed to the necessities of the occasion; and, as some of the spokes of the broken wheels were still whole, as well as parts of the rims it was soon decided that enough material for repairs was at hand, though we *were* "fifty miles from timber."

In a few hours the lost cattle were all recovered, and had plenty of time to rest and feed while the wagons were mended, which took all the remainder of that day, and the whole of the next. From this time for several days we went on, with nothing special to mark our progress, except passing the "Lone Tree," which I made into an event to myself by straining my eyes to get the first glimpse of it, watching its change from the first dim uncertainty, till it stood distinct in the distance, waiting our approach; then mentally holding converse with it as I drew near, questioning how it felt standing there all alone, not one of its kindred within sight! How long had it thus stood? What strange cause had led to its life of isolation? Had the thousands of human beings who had passed it before us, this season, cheered its old lone heart as their voices vibrated among its branches? Had any of them been cheered by observing its greenness, or resting in its shade? It was not a large tree, but its branches, covered with foliage, formed a well-rounded canopy for two or three. To me it was an impressive way-mark, which I passed with lingering steps, as I breathed silent thanksgivings for the "Hitherto" in which "the Lord had led us." As long as it remained in sight I cast frequent backward looks; feeling almost as though we were forsaking a living creature to the solitude of the desert.

July 1st at noon, we were camping near a large company whom we had overtaken when one or two horsemen came from the rear, with the information that the company to which they belonged, and which was very small, had become alarmed at the motions of some Indians who had made their appearance an hour or two before, and seemed preparing to attack them. The white men had, from a rising ground, seen the dust of our company ahead, and had sent to ask aid. Very promptly, 30 or 40 men from our company and the one near us, volunteered to answer the call, armed themselves and left us; while those remaining turned all the wagons into one corral and set guard. In two or three hours the others returned, with the report that the Indians had left, as soon as they saw superior numbers.

On the morning of July 4th we passed some remarkable rocks called Ancient Bluff Ruins, and came within sight of Chimney Rock, an immense natural tower visible for many miles before, and after, we passed it. In the afternoon we halted to celebrate the day. In one tent a few gathered for a dance; in another several of us old fashioned people enjoyed a cheerful "sing."

We were now within about a hundred miles of Fort Laramie and, in a day or two, began to look out for Laramie Peak. We first descried it as a faint cloud on the horizon, but the next day it became more distinct, and soon, its snow-covered top formed a cheering contrast to the monotony that had marked our view for so long. On the evening of July 9th we camped within three miles of Fort Laramie. Here we remained, resting, and recruiting [feeding and watering] the cattle, until the afternoon of the 11th when we crossed the Platt River, passed the Fort, near sunset, amid a glorious thunderstorm, and camped a mile and a half beyond. We now soon entered the Black Hills and the scenery became varied. July 15th we passed in the morning the northern foot of Laramie Peak, and saw a splendid thunderstorm circling about his venerable brow. At noon of the same day, we camped in a beautiful grove through which a clear mountain stream wound its way. It was a tempting place to tarry a while, and it seems we did not hurry to break up our mid-day halt; for I find in my diary a lengthened entry under that date, closing thus. "I have found a quiet spot at a little distance from the wagons, where I am seated on a stone, with book and pencil in hand, the babbling brook just at my feet, and close beside me, my little Mary, who is picking up the colored pebbles and throwing them, with exclamations of delight into the sparkling waters."

But these pleasant surroundings were exchanged, in a day or two, for a region of great scarcity of feed, the hills being originally not very productive, and the great numbers of cattle preceding us this summer, having eaten all feed near the road. The 17th of July, toward evening, we camped at Deer Creek, a branch of the Platt. The ground was utterly destitute of vegetation, though there were plenty of trees to give us shade. The men of the company now divided into two bands. The elderly ones, and the two or three having families, were detailed to stay with the wagons, keeping one or two horses with them; while the others, taking with them the other horses, drove the cattle up the creek valley, searching for food. They had to go 15 miles up the stream before they found a sufficiency; but there they came into a very rich valley, in which the poor animals luxuriated and rested for two days, communication being kept up between the two divisions of our company by means of the horses. Soon after resuming our journey we again crossed the Platt River to the north side. And now, once more, a terrific storm overtook us. Thunder, lightning, wind, hail and rain, poured their fury upon us. The terrified cattle were hastily detached from the wagons, and herded as near as possible to the leeside of a hill; but it was with the greatest difficulty they were kept from a stampede. This was on the 21st of July. A day or two afterward, we came upon the Sweetwater River, so named by Fremont and his men, on account of its waters being so much better than any they had tasted for several days before. It was indeed a pretty stream, and we began to ascend it with renewed spirits, knowing that when we reached its head we should soon pass the summit of the Rocky Mountains. July 26th we reached Independence Rock, where Fremont and his men spent the Fourth of July when they explored this route, and named the Rock accordingly. It is a bare mass of rock, without vegetation, rising directly from the flat, sandy land bordering the river, and detached entirely from any other elevation. Its general outline is round, though somewhat irregular; and at a distance one might fancy it an enormous elephant kneeling down. The least precipitous side was broken by irregular projections and narrow ledges, affording foothold for those willing to do some hard climbing. I had long before determined to ascend it, if I ever reached it, and found it not too rash an undertaking. Another woman of our company joined me. One or two of her boys climbed with us, and (just that she might have it to remember, and tell of) I took my little Mary. Of course I had to lift her from one projection to another most of the way; but we went leisurely, and her delight on reaching the top, our short rest there, and the view we enjoyed, fully paid for the labor.

On Sunday the 29th of July we determined to remain in camp and rest till the next day. One family of our fellow travelers Mr. B——. and his wife with their three little boys did the same. We enjoyed a quiet rest, held a social meeting for prayer, reading and singing, and the next morning resumed our journey, much refreshed. From this time till we reached Salt Lake we had no earthly company or protection except that mutually afforded and enjoyed by two men, two women and four children, the oldest not more than eight, and the youngest not yet three. Twice we met with Indians, but they did not molest us. We passed the company we had been traveling with, kept in advance of them, notwithstanding Sunday rests, and arrived in Salt Lake valley the day before they did.

But to return to our first week of lone traveling. For five days we kept on up the Sweetwater, and on Friday night encamped near its head. Not far from this, we made our nearest approach to the foot of Fremont Peak, of which we had a grand view as we walked beside our wagon. Saturday the 4th of August we reached the South Pass of the Rocky Mountains.

Our Guide Book gave very elaborate directions by which we might be able to identify the highest point in our road, where we passed from the Atlantic to the Pacific Slope. Otherwise we could not have noticed it, so gradual had been the ascent, and so slightly varied was the surface for a mile or two on all sides. But I had looked forward for weeks to the step that should take me past that point. In the morning of that day I had taken my last look at the waters that flowed eastward, to mingle with the streams and wash the shores where childhood and early youth had been spent; where all I loved, save O so small a number, lived; and now I stood on the almost imperceptible elevation that, when passed, would separate me from all these, perhaps forever. Through what toils and dangers we had come to reach that point; and, as I stood looking my farewell, a strong desire seized me to mark the spot in some way and record at least one word of grateful acknowledgement. Yes, I would make a little heap of stones, and mark on one of them, or on a stick, the word "Ebenezer."⁴ Nobody would notice or understand it; but my Heavenly Father would see the little monument in the mountain wilderness, and accept the humble thanks it recorded. So I turned to gather stones. But no stone could I find, not even pebbles enough to make a heap,—and no stick either, not a bush or a shrub or a tree within reach. So I stood still upon the spot till the two wagons and the little company had passed out of hearing, and when I left not a visible sign marked the place.

We were now for several days crossing the extreme northern end of the great Colorado Valley. Many of the springs were so strong with alkali as to be powerfully poisonous, and the grass in their vicinity was the same. One of our oxen died on the second day after entering this section, and we were obliged to yoke up the rest, and travel all night, so as to get to safer feed and water. On Saturday of that week we camped at night by Black Fork where we rested over Sunday. The next day reached Fort Bridger where was a rude log fort and one or two log huts. We got what information we could about the road and passed on. The next day Aug. 14th we crossed the dividing ridge between the Colorado Valley and the Great Salt Lake Basin. Here, in the Wasatch Mountains, our road was by far the most precipitous and the scenery the wildest we had yet seen. At the greatest elevation our altitude was seven thousand some hundred feet. Looking up to the high peak which towered above us on our left, we distinctly saw snow driving and eddying about in the strong wind. The clouds settled down nearer to us and we had a lively sprinkling of rain for a short time; but as we descended we were soon again in the hot sunshine; the dust, which had been excessive for two days, growing deeper and deeper, lighter and lighter, till it was like wading through a bed of fine ashes; so that when, at the entrance of Great Salt Lake Valley, we paused to take breath, and faced each other with mutual looks of wonder, we agreed that we did not know each other; and it was not till after a free use of the pure valley waters, aided in some instances by the hot mineral springs, that we recovered our identity.

It was near sunset on the 18th of August when we got our first view of the Great Salt Lake, with its background of mountains; and in its foreground the well-laid-out city of snug dwellings and thrifty gardens. The suddenness with which we came upon the view was startling. From narrow mountain gorges and rough crooked turns, our road abruptly led us through an opening, almost like an immense doorway, unarched at the top. Here we were on a small plateau some hundreds of feet above the valley, with nothing to obstruct our view for many miles. It is impossible to describe how, in the transparent atmosphere, everything was brought out with a distinctness that almost ignored distance. From here the road wound gradually down the mountainside to the plain and then into the City. As it was near sunset we camped on the second plateau, rested there through Sunday, and then moved into the City of Great Salt Lake. At this point, company organizations were broken up, almost without exception, and every man proceeded to make such arrangements as seemed best to himself and those belonging to the same wagon. In many cases, even those owning teams and wagons together, sold out and parted goods, each taking his own way. Some few hurried on at once, but nearly all remained, a few days at least, to recruit. There was a general selling of tired-out cattle; and buying of fresh. Soon, notice was formally circulated among the emigrants that a certain man, whose name I forget, professing to be an experienced traveler, and explorer of the Great Basin, would lead a company to California by a route far south of the one followed by emigrants thus far. He would start from Salt Lake City a month or two later, and he strongly advised tired travelers to remain and rest themselves, and then join his party. We heard all this, and discussed it. We also heard the warnings, and saw the solemnly shaken heads of the Mormon Prophets.

They told us we would lose our cattle and perish on the desert; or, if we reached the Sierras would be snowed in, and perish there. We heard it, we coolly talked it over, and yet, so perverse were we, that on the 30th day of August, a solitary wagon, drawn by three yoke of oxen and in charge of only two men, left Salt Lake City, bearing as its passengers, one woman and one little child, and for freight only so much provision as might last us till we could scale the great Sierras and reach their western foot.

Our only guide from Salt Lake City consisted of two small sheets of note paper, sewed together, and bearing on the outside in writing the title "Best Guide to the Gold Mines, 816 miles, by Ira J. Willes, GSL City." This little pamphlet was wholly in writing, there being at that time no printing press at Salt Lake. It was gotten up by a man who had been to California and back the preceding year. The directions, and the descriptions of camping places, together with the distances, seemed pretty definite and satisfactory until they reached the lower part of the Mary's or Humboldt River; when poor camping and scarcity of water were mentioned with discouraging frequency. From the sink of the Humboldt, all seemed confusion. We were told by our writer, to look out for a new track which "was to be made last fall" and which "*might be* better," and just here, for several stages, all seemed uncertainty. Indeed the man from whom we got the Guide Book told my husband he must be guided in this part of the way by information which he must get from a returning Mormon Train, which we would meet before reaching the Humboldt.

The only man who now accompanied my husband was considerably advanced in years, and not in perfect health. He was extremely anxious to reach California, but had no means in the world save one solitary ox, a little clothing, and sufficient food to sustain him till he reached El Dorado, if he could go straight through. He offered to put his ox into the team, to help drive and take care of the cattle, and assist otherwise, so far as able, for the privilege of traveling in company, and having his few things carried.

Thus we set forth on the last, and by far the most perilous, stage of our great journey. We had traveled but a few days, when, after camping one evening, we saw approaching, a couple of young men, scarcely beyond boyhood, having with them a horse and a mule. They stopped not far from us, turned out their animals to feed, made a fire and took their evening meal, as we were doing; and, after awhile, came over to our camp to talk. They also had launched out alone and would be very glad to keep in company with us. As they appeared civil, and one of them rather gentlemanly, we of course did not object. This seemed like a little more protection; but it had its drawbacks; for we soon found out they had very little to eat; and in a few days they began to plead for some of our flour; promising they would hunt, away from the road, every day and bring in game to keep up the supply of provisions. But game was scarce, and very few were the times along the whole way that they caught any. We had allowed a very small margin of provisions for contingencies because the necessity for the fastest possible traveling was so great. Still we kept on, sharing, and hoping for the best. Their efforts at hunting, fruitless as they usually were, kept the young men away from the road most of the time, so that we were nearly as much alone as ever.

On the morning of the 11th of September they had been away from us for some hours, we were moving quietly along our way, no living creature, save our plodding team and our own feeble company, within sight, when, suddenly, there appeared from between the hills a party of Indians. As they came nearer we saw they were all armed; and presently several arranged themselves in a sort of semi circle closing the road, and one of them laid his rifle across the foreheads of our leaders, and stopped the team. From my seat in the wagon I had from their first appearance observed every movement. I saw we were completely in their power. Their numbers and their arms were enough to destroy us in a few moments. Even if the young men with their guns were at hand there would be no hope in battle. If firing once commenced those savages would not cease till they had laid low, at least, every man of the company. There was no hope, save in an influence that should change their purpose, in so far as it was hostile, and supply motives for letting us go. With my whole soul, I prayed that God would wield that influence, and supply those motives; and as they closed around us I cast all into His hands without any other hope. At first every appearance was hostile. They were importunate in demanding various things, acted with the air of victors, some of the younger ones pressed close to the wagons, and looked in, with boisterous exclamations, and impertinent gestures. But I was enabled to keep a firm unblanching front, taking care that my little Mary did not stir from my side. She was too young to realize any danger, and thought the whole rather amusing. My husband met them from the first with a calm, business-like air, as if he thought they wanted to hold a consultation with him; and when they became overbearing, he still kept on making speeches to them, though we could not perceive that they understood what he said. Their behavior changed several times quite strangely. They would draw nearer together and consult with puzzled looks, some of them still guarding the team. Then they would scowl and seem to differ among themselves. Thus they kept us for perhaps an hour, when, all at once, my husband raised the big ox-whip, shouted to the cattle, and rushed them forward so suddenly that those nearest

Indians instinctively stepped aside, then pompously exclaiming, "I'm going to move on," he called the old man to follow, and we were once more in motion. But would they let us keep on? I looked through a small gap in the wagon. They were evidently puzzled by such unusual behavior, and as evidently divided in their counsels. Some were vociferating, with their guns in threatening positions, others plainly differed from them, but it was certain they had not quite decided what to do, when a turn of the road took us out of sight. We expected they would way-lay us again; for we were passing through several narrow defiles that day,—but the hours went by and night came, without another sight of the enemy. My husband kept guard that night, and I slept very little. The others of our little company disappeared among the bushes and seemed to sleep as well as usual.

Two days after this we met a band of Mormons who had been gold hunting in California for the summer, and were on their return to Salt Lake. This was the company whose leader was to tell us how we might get from the Sink of the Humboldt, otherwise Mary's River, to Carson River; for that was a part of our journey which yet lay shrouded in grim mystery. The directions given us seemed very plain. He traced out the road in the sand with a stick,—I think it was his whip-handle. It was taken for granted that we knew our way to the "Sink of Mary's River" so he took *that* for his starting point in giving us directions; and showed us that, soon after passing there, we would see a plain wagon track leading to the left, which we were to follow, and it would bring us to grassy meadows, lying two or three miles from the main road, and so, still abounding in feed. Here also, he said, we would find several shallow wells, dug but recently, in the last part of the season, by Mormons, who had gone to spend the winter in California, and on their way there had found these meadows, cut feed in them for use on the 40 mile desert and, on arriving in California, had given to him and his company,—then just about to start for Salt Lake,—directions to find the spot. The wells, he said, had good water in them when he was there a few days before. None of them were deep, but the water was near the surface all about there, and we could, if we found it desirable, scoop out one or two of the holes deeper, let them settle all night, and in the morning have plenty of fresh water. He was evidently an old and experienced traveler of deserts, plains and mountains. He advised us to camp in the meadows he described, for at least two or three days, let the cattle rest and feed freely, while the men made it their first business to cut as much hay as there was room for in the wagon. This would partly dry while the cattle were recruiting; then load it up, fill every available vessel with water, and set out on the desert about noon of the day, if the weather were cool,—otherwise toward evening. When once out on the desert we were to stop at intervals of a few hours, feed some of the hay to the cattle, give them a moderate drink, let them breathe a short time and then go on. In this way, he said, we would be able to reach Carson river in about 24 hours from the time of starting on the desert. After hearing his instructions, and having the road made thus plain to us, we went on with renewed cheerfulness and energy. On Sunday the 16th of September we camped on the head branch of Mary's River, and on Monday morning passed through a cañon which brought us to the River itself, down which we continued to travel for several days.

It was now getting late in the season, and we could not help feeling it rather ominous that a thunder-storm overtook us one evening; followed by cold nights; and on the evening and night of the 1st of October a terrific wind blew, threatening for hours to strangle us with thick clouds of sand, and to blow our wagon, with all our means of living, over the steep bluff. But a good Providence preserved us and, with the morning, calm returned. We had now nearly reached the head of Humboldt Lake, which, at this late period in the dry season, was utterly destitute of water, the river having sunk gradually in the sand, until, hereabout, it entirely disappeared. Still, the name, "Sink of Mary's or Humboldt River" was applied in our Guide Book, as well as in conversations at Salt Lake City, to the *southern* or *lower end* of Humboldt Lake, a point some ten miles farther on our way. Where, we were told, there were several holes dug close to the road. Having always understood it to be thus applied, it of course never came into our minds to suppose, that our Mormon friend, when he so particularly marked in the sand "The Sink of Mary's," meant the point where *at that time* the river *actually disappeared*. When, therefore, on the night

of October 2nd, we camped in the neighborhood of the last mentioned point; we said, "Now, we must be about twelve or thirteen
miles from where that road to the meadows leads off to the left;
and thence it will be only two or three miles to the meadows,
where we are to rest and prepare for the desert. If we rise *very
early* tomorrow morning, we shall get there by noon, and have
a half day to settle camp, and get ready for work." Accordingly,
the first one who woke the next morning roused all the rest, and,
though we found it was not much past two o'clock, we agreed it
was not best to sleep again; so by our fire of sage-brush, we took
some hot coffee, and the last bit of rabbit pot-pie,—the result of
a very rare success the day before,—yoked up the oxen, and went
resolutely on our way. It was moonlight, but the gray-white sand
with only here and there a sage-bush looked all so much alike
that it required care to keep the road. And now, for the first time
in my life, I saw a mirage; or rather several repetitions of that
optical illusion. Once it was an extended sheet of water lying
calmly bright in the moonlight, with here and there a tree on its
shores; and our road seemed to tend directly towards it; then it
was a small lake seen through openings in a row of trees, while
the shadowy outlines of a forest appeared beyond it; all lying
to our left. What a pity it seemed to be passing it by, when our
poor animals had been so stinted of late. Again, we were traveling parallel with a placid river on our right, beyond which were
trees; and from us to the water's edge the ground sloped so gently
it appeared absurd not to turn aside to its brink and refresh ourselves and our oxen. But, as day dawned, these beautiful sights
disappeared, and we began to look anxiously for the depression
in the ground, and the holes dug, which we were told would mark
the Sink of the Humboldt. But it was nearly noonday before we
came to them. There was still some passable water in the holes
but not fit to drink clear; so we contrived to gather enough sticks
of sage to boil some, made a little coffee, ate our lunch and, thus
refreshed, we hastened to find the forking road. Our director had
told us, that within about two or three miles beyond the Sink we
might look for the road, to the left, and we did look, and kept
looking, and going on, drearily till the sun got lower and lower,
and night was fast approaching.

Then, the conviction, which had long been gaining ground in my mind, took possession of the whole party. We had passed the forks of the road before daylight that morning, and were now miles out on the desert without a mouthful of feed for the cattle and only two or three quarts of water in a little cask. What could be done? Halt we must, for the oxen were nearly worn out, and night was coming on. The animals must at least *rest*, if they could not be fed; and, that they might rest, they were chained securely to the wagon; for, hungry and thirsty as they were, they would, if loose, start off frantically in search of water and food, and soon drop down exhausted. Having fastened them in such a way that they could lie down, we took a few mouthfuls of food, and then, we in our wagon and the men not far off upon the sand, fell wearily to sleep; a forlorn little company *wrecked upon the desert*. The first question in the morning was, "How can the oxen be kept from starving?" A happy thought occurred. We had, thus far on our journey, managed to keep something in the shape of a bed to sleep on. It was a mattress-tick, and, just before leaving Salt Lake, we had put into it some fresh hay,—not very much, for our load must be as light as possible; but the old gentleman traveling with us had also a small straw mattress; the two together might keep the poor things from starving for a few hours. At once, a small portion was dealt out to them and for the present they were saved. For ourselves we had food which we believed would about last us till we reached the Gold Mines if we could go right on; if we were much delayed anywhere, it was doubtful. The two or three quarts of water in our little cask would last only a few hours to give very moderate drinks to each of the party. For myself I inwardly determined I should scarcely take any of it, as I had found, throughout the journey, that I could do with less drink than most land travelers. Some of the men, however, easily suffered with thirst, and, as to my little girl, it is well known, a child cannot do long without either water or milk. Everything looked rather dark and dubious. Should we try to go on? But there were miles of desert before us, in which, we knew, neither grass or water could be found. We had been told by those who had crossed it with comparatively fresh teams, that, with plenty of hay and water to bait with, we might get over it in about 24 hours though it was acknowledged it might take us longer. Here we were, without water, and with only a few mouthfuls of poor feed, while our animals were already tired out, and very hungry and thirsty. No, it would be madness to go farther out in the desert under such conditions. Should we then turn back and try to reach the meadows with their wells? But, as near as we could calculate it, it could not be less than twelve or fifteen miles to them. Would it be possible for our poor cattle to reach there? Their only food would be that pitiful mess still left in our mattresses. It might be divided into two portions, giving them each a few mouthfuls more at noon; and then, if they kept on their feet long enough to reach the holes at the Sink, we might possibly find enough water to give them each a little drink, which, with the remainder of the fodder *might* keep them up till the meadows were reached. It was a forlorn hope, but it was all we had. The morning was wearing away while these things were talked over. Precious time was being wasted; but the truth was, the situation was so new and unexpected that it seemed for awhile to confuse, almost to stupefy, most of the little party; and, those least affected in this way, felt so deeply the responsibility of the next move, that they dared not decide upon it hastily. The least responsible and efficient of the company had been, most of the morning, wandering aimlessly about, sometimes keeping within a small circle, then again branching off nearly out of sight. Perhaps they all had a vague hope they might find another track. But now, as noon approached, they gathered near the wagon, tired, moody, and evidently very near "giving up." But this would never do. So the more hopeful ones proposed that we should all eat something and, as soon as the noon heat abated, prepare for a move. So we took some lunch, and soon the men were lying upon the sand at short distances from each other, fast asleep. My little Mary slept too. But I was not sleepy. With unwearied gaze my eyes swept, again and again, the shimmering horizon. There was no help or hope there. Then I looked at what lay nearest. How short-lived our few remaining resources would be, unless fresh strength came soon from somewhere. How still it was. Only the sound of a few feeble breaths. It would not take many hours of starvation to quiet them forever. All the human aid we had could do but little now, and if, in trying to do that little, one more mistake were made, it must be fatal. Whence then this calm strength which guided me round so surely, while I, and all surrounding me were so weak? I had known what it was to *believe* in God, and to pray that He would never leave us. Was it thus then that when all other helpers failed, He came so near that I no longer simply *believed* in Him, but *knew* His presence there, giving strength for whatever might come?

Soon some of the party awoke and, after a little talk, concluded that two of them would walk to a bald ridge that rose out of the flat waste, about a mile and a half distant, and take a view from thence, in the faint hope that we might yet be mistaken, and the forking road and the meadows might still be in advance. My husband said he would go, and the best of the two young men went with him while the other two wandered listlessly off again. I made no opposition; I felt no inclination to oppose; though I knew the helplessness and loneliness of the position would thus be greatly increased. But that calm strength, that certainty of One near and all sufficient hushed and cheered me. Only a woman who has been alone upon a desert with her helpless child can have any adequate idea of my experience for the next hour or two. But that consciousness of an unseen Presence still sustained me. When the explorers returned from their walk to the ridge, it was only to report, no discovery, nothing to be seen on all sides but sand and scattered sagebrush interspersed with the carcasses of dead cattle. So there was nothing to be done but to turn back and try to find the meadows. Turn back! What a chill the words sent through one. *Turn back*, on a journey like that; in which every mile had been gained by most earnest labor, growing more and more intense, until, of late, it had seemed that the certainty of advance with every step, was all that made the next step possible. And now for miles we were to *go back*. In all that long journey no steps ever seemed so heavy, so hard to take, as those with which I turned my back to the sun that afternoon of October 4th 1849.

We had not been long on the move when we saw dust rising in the road at a distance and soon perceived we were about to meet a little caravan of wagons. Then a bright gleam of hope stole in. They had doubtless stopped at the meadows, and were supplied with grass and water. Might it not be possible that they would have enough to spare for us? Then we could go on with them. My heart bounded at the thought. But the hope was short lived. We met, and some of the men gathered round our wagon with eager inquiries, while those who could not leave their teams stood looking, with wonder, at a solitary wagon headed the wrong way. Our story was soon told. It turned out that they were camping in the meadows at the very time we passed the forking road without seeing it, the morning we so ambitiously started soon after midnight. Ah, we certainly got up too early that day. If we had only seen that road and taken it, we might now have been with this company, provided for the desert, and no longer alone. But, when the question was asked whether they could spare sufficient grass and water to get our team over the desert, they shook their heads and unanimously agreed that it was out of the question. Their own cattle, they said, were weak from long travel, and too often scant supplies. They had only been able to load up barely enough to get to the Carson river. The season was far advanced and the clouds, hanging of late round the mountain tops, looked threatening. It would be like throwing away their own lives without any certainty of saving ours; for once out in the desert without food we would all be helpless together. One of the men had his family with him, a wife and two or three children; and while they talked the woman was seen coming towards us. She had not, when they first halted, understood that any but men were with the lone wagon. As soon as she heard to the contrary, and what were the circumstances, she hastened, with countenance full of concern, to condole with me, and, I think, had the decision depended alone upon her, she would have insisted upon our turning back with them and sharing their feed and water to the last. But fortunately for them, probably for us all, other counsels prevailed, and we resumed our depressing backward march.

Two or three things, before uncertain, were settled by this meeting. The first was the distance to the meadows, which they agreed could not be less than 14 or 16 miles from where we met them, which seems, in our circumstances, like an appalling interval. But there was relief in being assured that we should find a pretty good supply of water in the holes at the Sink, where we were to camp that night, and that, when we once reached the meadows, there was food and water enough for a number of teams during many days. We had also definite directions as to the shortest road, and were assured it was perfectly plain and good except that it was rather sandy. I had now become so impressed with the danger of the cattle giving out that I refused to ride except for occasional brief rests. So, soon after losing sight of the dust of the envied little caravan, I left the wagon and walked the remainder of the day. For a good while I kept near the wagon but, by and by, being very weary I fell behind. The sun had set before we reached the Sink, and the light was fading fast when the wagon disappeared from my sight behind a slight elevation; and, as the others had gone on in advance some time before, I was all alone on the barren waste. However, as I recognized the features of the neighborhood, and knew we were quite near the Sink, I felt no particular apprehension, only a feeling that it was a weird and dreary scene, and instinctively urged forward my lagging footsteps in hope of regaining sight of the wagon. Suddenly I caught sight of an object a few rods distant on the left of the road, moving steadily but rather stealthily toward the road, in a line that would intercept it some paces ahead of me. I stopped, the creature stopped too, looking steadily at me. It was a Coyote. I had several times during the journey heard them howling at night but, as the season had advanced, they had been seldom heard, and to meet one thus almost face to face with no human being in sight was a little startling. But, calling to mind what I had heard of their reluctance to face a steady look and determined resistance, I lifted my hands with threatening gestures, raised a shout, and sprang forward a step or two. Mr. Coyote stood a moment as if questioning the resistance offered; but when I repeated, more violently, the gestures and the shouts, he turned and retraced his steps into the dim distance, only looking back once or twice to see if the enemy retained the ground. As he disappeared I hastened forward, and in a few minutes came within sight of the wagon, now halted for the night near the camp-fire, which the men had just lit.

The next morning we resumed our backward march after feeding out the last mouthful of fodder. The water in the little cask was nearly used up in making coffee for supper and breakfast; but, if only each one would be moderate in taking a share when thirst impelled him, we might yet reach the wells before any one suffered seriously. We had lately had but few chances for cooking; and only a little boiled rice with dried fruit, and a few bits of biscuit remained after we had done breakfast. If we could only reach the meadows by noon. But that we could hardly hope for, the animals were so weak and tired. There was no alternative however, the only thing to be done was to go steadily on, determined to do and endure to the utmost. I found no difficulty this morning in keeping up with the team. They went so slowly, and I was so preternaturally stimulated by anxiety to get forward, that, before I was aware of it I would be some rods ahead of the cattle, straining my gaze as if expecting to see a land of promise, long before I had any rational hope of the kind. My imagination acted intensely. I seemed to see Hagar in the wilderness, walking wearily away from her fainting child among the dried up bushes, and seating herself in the hot sand. I seemed to become Hagar myself, and when my little one, from the wagon behind me, called out, "Mamma I want a drink,"—I stopped, gave her some, noted that there were but a few swallows left, then mechanically pressed onward again, alone, repeating, over and over, the words "Let me not see the death of the child."[5] Just in the heat of noon-day we came to where the sage bushes were nearer together and a fire, left by campers or Indians, had spread for some distance, leaving beds of ashes, and occasionally charred skeletons of bushes to make the scene more dreary. Smoke was still sluggishly curling up here and there, but no fire was visible; when, suddenly just before me to my right a bright flame sprang up at the foot of a small bush, ran rapidly up it, leaped from one little branch to another till all, for a few seconds, were ablaze together, then went out, leaving nothing but a few ashes and a little smoldering trunk. It was a small incident, easily accounted for, but to my then over-wrought fancy it made more vivid the illusion of being a wanderer in a far off, old-time desert, and myself witnessing a wonderful phenomenon. For a few moments I stood with bowed head worshiping the God of Horeb, and I was strengthened thereby.[6]

Wearily passed the hottest noon-day hour, with many an anxious look at the horned-heads, which seemed to me to bow lower and lower, while the poor tired hoofs almost refused to move. The two young men had been out of sight for sometime; when, all at once, we heard a shout, and saw, a few hundred yards in advance, a couple of hats thrown into the air and four hands waving triumphantly. As soon as we got near enough, we heard them call out, "Grass and water! Grass and water!" and shortly we were at the meadows. The remainder of that day was spent chiefly in rest and refreshment. The next day the men busied themselves in cutting and spreading grass; while I sorted out and rearranged things in the wagon so as to make all possible room for hay and water; and also cooked all the meat we had left, and as much of our small stock of flour, rice and dried fruit, as might last us till we could again find wood.

The day after that was Sunday, and we should have had a very quiet rest, had we not been visited by a party of some eight or ten Indians, who came from the Humboldt Mountains on Saturday afternoon and remained near us till we left. They professed to be friendly; but were rather troublesome, and evidently desirous of getting something out of us if they could. Two or three of them had rifles; and when the young men went to talk to them they began to show off their marksmanship by firing at particular objects. The young men felt this to be rather of the nature of a challenge; and thought it would be safer to accept than to ignore it. So they got the arms from the wagon, set up a mark, and, as one of them—the gentleman of the two—proved to be a remarkable shot, the Indians were struck with surprise, which, as, time after time, W——.'s ball hit within an inch of his aim, grew to admiration, and ended in evident awe; for not one of their party could quite equal him. How much our safety and exemption from pillage were due to that young man's true aim, we might not be quite sure, but I have always been very willing to acknowledge a debt of gratitude to him.

On Monday morning we loaded up, but did not hurry, for the cattle had not rested any too long; another day would have been better, but we dared not linger. So, giving them time that morning to thoroughly satisfy themselves with grass and water we once more set forward toward the formidable desert, and, at that late season, with our equipment, the scarcely less formidable Sierras.

The feeling that we were once more going forward instead of backward gave an animation to every step which we could never have felt but by contrast. By night we were again at the Sink where we once more camped; but we durst not, the following morning, launch out upon the desert with the whole day before us; for though it was now the 9th of October, the sun was still powerful for some hours daily, and the arid sand doubled its heat. Not much after noon, however, we ventured out upon the sea of sand, this time to cross or die. Not far from the edge of night we stopped to bait [eat and drink], at no great distance from the scene of our last week's bitter disappointment. Once beyond that, I began to feel renewed courage as though the worst were passed; and, as I had walked much of the afternoon, and knew I must walk again by and by, I was persuaded to get into the wagon and lie down by Mary, who was sleeping soundly. By a strong effort of will, backed by the soothing influence of prayer, I fell asleep, but only for a few minutes. I was roused by the stopping of the wagon, and then my husband's voice said, "So you've given out, have you Tom?" and at the same moment I knew by the rattling chains and yokes that some of the cattle were being loosed from the team. I was out of the wagon in a minute. One of the oxen was prostrate on the ground, and his companion, from whose neck the yoke was just being removed, looked very likely soon to follow him. It had been the weak couple all along. Now we had but two yoke. How soon would they, one by one, follow? Nothing could induce me to get into the wagon again. I said I would walk by the team, and for awhile I did; but by and by I found myself yards ahead. An inward power urged me forward; and the poor cattle were so slow, it seemed every minute as if they were going to stop. When I got so far off as to miss the sound of footsteps and wheels, I would pause, startled, wait and listen, dreading lest they had stopped, then as they came near I would again walk beside them awhile, watching, through the darkness, the dim outlines of their heads and horns to see if they drooped lower. But soon I found myself again forward and alone.

There was no moon yet, but by starlight we had for sometime seen, only too plainly, the dead bodies of cattle lying here and there on both sides of the road. As we advanced they increased in number, and presently we saw two or three wagons. At first we thought we had overtaken a company, but coming close no sign of life appeared. We had candles with us, so, as there was not the least breeze we lit one or two and examined. Everything indicated a complete break down, and a hasty flight. Some animals were lying nearly in front of a wagon, apparently just as they had dropped down, while loose yokes and chains indicated that part of the teams had been driven on, laden probably with some necessaries of life; for the contents of the wagons were scattered in confusion, the most essential articles alone evidently having been thought worth carrying. "Ah," we said, "some belated little company has been obliged to pack what they could, and hurry to the river. Maybe it was the little company we met the other day." It was not a very encouraging scene but our four oxen still kept their feet; we would drive on a little farther, out of this scene of ruin, bait them, rest ourselves and go on. We did so, but soon found that what we had supposed an exceptional misfortune must have been the common fate of many companies; for at still shortening intervals, scenes of ruin similar to that just described kept recurring till we seemed to be but the last little, feeble, struggling band at the rear of a routed army. From near midnight on through the small hours, it appeared necessary to stop more frequently, for both man and beast were sadly weary, and craved frequent nourishment. Soon after midnight we finished the last bit of meat we had; but there was still enough of the biscuit, rice and dried fruit to give us two or three more little baits. The waning moon now gave us a little melancholy light, showing still the bodies of dead cattle, and the forms of forsaken wagons as our grim waymarks. In one or two instances they had been left in the very middle of the road; and we had to turn out into the untracked sand to pass them. Soon we came upon a scene of wreck that surpassed anything preceding it. As we neared it, we wondered at the size of the wagons which, in the dim light, looked tall as houses against the sky. Coming to them, we found three or four of them to be of the make that the early Mississippi Valley emigrants used to call "Prairie Schooners," having deep beds, with projecting backs and high tops. One of them was specially immense, and, useless as we felt it to be to spend time in examining these warning relics of those who had gone before us, curiosity led us to lift the front curtain, which hung down, and by the light of our candle that we had again lit, look in. There, from the strong, high bows hung several sides of well-cured bacon much better in quality than that we had finished at our last resting place. So we had but a short interval in which to say we were destitute of meat; for, though warned by all we saw not to add a useless pound to our load, we thought it wise to take a little, to eke out our scanty supply of food. And, as to the young men, who had so rarely, since they joined us, had a bit of meat they could call their own, they were very glad to bear the burden of a few pounds of bacon slung over their shoulders. After this little episode, the only cheering incident for many hours, we turned to look at what lay round these monster wagons. It would be impossible to describe the motley collections of things of various sorts, strewed all about. The greater part of the materials, however, were pasteboard boxes, some complete, but most of them broken, and pieces of wrapping paper still creased, partially in the form of packages. But the most prominent objects were two or three, per-haps more, very beautifully finished trunks of various sizes, some of them standing open, their pretty trays lying on the ground and all rifled of their contents; save that occasionally a few pamphlets, or, here and there, a book remained in the corners. We concluded that this must have been a company of merchants hauling a load of goods to California, that some of their animals had given out, and, fearing the rest would, they had packed such things as they could, and had fled for their lives toward the river. There was only one thing (besides the few pounds of bacon) that, in all these varied heaps of things many of which, in civilized scenes, would have been valuable, I thought worth picking up. That was a little book, bound in cloth and illustrated with a number of small engravings. Its title was "Little Ella." I thought it would please Mary, so I put it in my pocket. It was an easily-carried souvenir of the desert; and more than one pair of young eyes learned to read its pages in after years.

Morning was now approaching, and we hoped, when full daylight came, to see some signs of the river. But for two or three weary hours after sunrise nothing of the kind appeared. The last of the water had been given to the cattle before daylight. When the sun was up we gave them the remainder of their hay, took a little breakfast and pressed forward. For a long time not a word was spoken save occasionally to the cattle. I had again, unconsciously, got in advance; my eyes scanning the horizon to catch the first glimpse of any change; though I had no definite idea in my mind what first to expect. But now there was surely something. Was it a cloud? It was very low at first and I feared it might evaporate as the sun warmed it. But it became rather more distinct and a little higher. I paused and stood till the team came up. Then walking beside it I asked my husband what he thought that low dark line could be. "I think," he said, "it must be timber on Carson River." Again we were silent and for a while I watched anxiously the heads of the two leading cattle. They were rather unusually fine animals, often showing considerable intelligence, and so faithful had they been, through so many trying scenes, I could not help feeling a sort of attachment to them; and I pitied them, as I observed how low their heads drooped as they pressed their shoulders so resolutely and yet so wearily against the bows. Another glance at the horizon. Surely there was now visible a little unevenness in the top of that dark line, as though it might indeed be trees. "How far off do you think that is now?" I said. "About five or six miles I guess," was the reply. At that moment the white-faced leader raised his head, stretched forward his nose and uttered a low "Mooooo." I was startled, fearing it was the sign for him to fall, exhausted. "What is the matter with him?" I said. "I think he smells the water," was the answer. "How can he at such a distance?" As I spoke, the other leader raised his head, stretched out his nose, and uttered the same sound. The hinder cattle seemed to catch the idea, whatever it was; they all somewhat increased their pace, and from that time, showed renewed animation. But we had yet many weary steps to take, and noon had passed before we stood in the shade of those longed-for trees, beside the Carson River. As soon as the yokes were removed the oxen walked into the stream and stood a few moments, apparently enjoying its coolness, then drank as they chose, came out, and soon found feed that satisfied them for the present, though at this point it was not abundant. The remainder of that day was spent in much needed rest.

The next day we did not travel many miles, for our team showed decided signs of weakness, and the sand became deeper as we advanced, binding the wheels so as to make hauling very hard. We had conquered the desert; but the great Sierra Nevada Mountains were still all before us, and we had many miles to make, up this River, before their ascent was fairly begun. If this sand continued many miles as looked probable, when should we ever even begin the real climbing? The men began to talk among themselves about how much easier they could get on if they left the wagon; and it was not unlikely they would try starting out without us if we had to travel too slowly. But they could not do this to any real advantage unless they took with them their pack-mule to carry some provisions. All they had was the bacon they found on the desert and some parched cornmeal; but they felt sanguine that they could go so much faster than the cattle with the wagon, they could easily make this last them through. But the bargain had been, when we agreed to supply them with flour, that the pack mule, and the old horse if he could be of any use, should be at our service to aid in any pinch that might occur, to the end of the journey. Having shared the perils of the way thus far, it certainly seemed unwise to divide the strength of so small a party when the mountains were to be scaled.

I wished most heartily there was some more rapid way for Mary and me to ride. But it was out of the question; for, only a thoroughly trained mountain animal would do for me to ride carrying her. Besides this, all the clothing and personal conveniences we had in the world were in our wagon, and we had neither a sufficient number of sound animals nor those of the right kind, to pack them across the mountains. So the only way was to try to keep on. But it looked like rather a hopeless case when, for this whole day, we advanced but a few miles.

The next morning, Friday the 12th of October, we set out once more, hoping the sand would become lighter and the road easier to travel. But, instead of this, the wheels sank deeper than yesterday, there was more of ascent to overcome, the sun shone out decidedly hot, and, towards noon, we saw that we were approaching some pretty steep hills up which our road evidently led. It did not look as though we could ascend them but we would at least try to reach their foot. As we neared them we saw dust rising from the road at one of the turns we could distinguish high up in the hills a few miles off. Probably it was some party ahead of us. There was no hope of our overtaking anybody, so when we lost sight of the dust we did not expect to see it again. But soon another section of the road was in sight, and again the dust appeared, this time nearer, and plainly moving towards us. Conjecture now became very lively. It was probably Indians; but they could not be of the same tribes we had seen. Were they foes? How many were there? Repeatedly we saw the dust at different points but could make out no distinct figures. We were now so near the foot of the hills that we could distinctly see a stretch of road leading down a very steep incline to where we were moving so laboriously along. Presently at the head of this steep incline appeared two horsemen, clad in loose, flying garments that flapped like wings on each side of them, while their broad-brimmed hats blown up from their foreheads, revealed hair and faces that belonged to no Indians. Their rapidity of motion and the steepness of the descent gave a strong impression of coming down from above, and the thought flashed into my mind, "They look heaven sent." As they came nearer we saw that each of them led by a halter a fine mule, and the perfect ease with which all the animals cantered down that steep, was a marvel in our eyes. My husband and myself were at the heads of the lead cattle, and our little Mary was up in the front of the wagon, looking with wonder at the approaching forms. As they came near they smiled and the forward one said, "Well sir, you are the man we are after!" "How can that be?" said my husband, with surprise. "Yes, sir," continued the stranger, "you and your wife, and that little girl are what brought us as far as this. You see we belong to the Relief Company sent out by order of the United States Government to help the late emigrants over the mountains. We were ordered only as far as Truckee Pass. When we got there we met a little company that had just got in. They'd been in a snow storm at the summit; 'most got froze to death themselves, lost some of their cattle, and just managed to get to where some of our men had fixed a relief camp. There was a woman and some children with them, and that woman set right to work at us fellows to go on over the mountains after a family she said they'd met on the desert going back for grass and water 'cause they'd missed their way. She said there was only one wagon, and there was a woman and child in it; and she knew they could never get through them canyons and over them ridges without help. We told her we had no orders to go any farther then. She said she did not care for orders. She didn't believe anybody would blame us for doing what we were sent out to do, if we did have to go farther than ordered. And she kept at me so, I couldn't get rid of her. You see I've got a wife and little girl of my own; so I felt just how it was; and I got this man to come with me and here we are to give you more to eat, if you want it, let you have these two mules, and tell you how to get right over the mountains the best and quickest way."

While he thus rapidly, in cheery though blunt fashion, explained their sudden presence with us, the thought of their being heaven-sent, that had so lightly flashed into my mind as I at first watched their rapid descent of the hill, with flying garments, grew into a sweetly solemn conviction; and I stood in mute adoration, breathing, in my inmost heart, thanksgiving to that Providential Hand which had taken hold of the conflicting movements, the provoking blunders, the contradictory plans of our lives, and those of a dozen other people, who a few days before were utterly unknown to each other, and many miles apart, and had from those rough, broken materials wrought out for us so unlooked-for a deliverance. Having made their hasty explanation, our new friends advised us to keep on some little distance farther, to a point where there was a spring in the hills, and excellent camping, to which they would guide us. There we were to rest the remainder of the day, while they would help to select, put into proper shape and pack, everything in the wagon that could be packed. The rest we must be content to leave. As we moved leisurely on to our camping place, they explained more fully the details of our situation, which they understood so much better than we could, and told us what we were to do. There had been two nights of snow-storm at the summit; had there come much more they could not have got through. But the weather had cleared, the snow was fast going off the roads as they came over; and, if no other storm occurred, the pass would be in good order when we reached it. But we must hasten with all possible dispatch, for, when the storms once again set in, they were not likely at that season to give any more chance for crossing the mountains. As to keeping on with the wagon, even supposing the cattle to grow no weaker than now, it would take us two weeks at the least to ascend the Carson Valley to the cañon. That cañon could not in several places be traversed by wheels. Wagons had been taken through, but only by taking them apart and packing, at the most difficult points, which of course could only be done by strong companies with plenty of time. Our only hope, therefore, was to pack. They then went farther into details about packing. The oxen, they said, could easily be made to carry, each, two moderate sized bundles, if snugly packed and well fastened on. Then the old horse could carry something though not very much. And the mule the young men had brought along, they said must carry most of the provisions. "And now as to these two mules we brought," continued the chief speaker, "this white one is a perfectly-trained, mountain, saddle-mule. My wife has rode him for miles, over steep and slippery roads, and he'll be perfectly safe for this lady to ride, with her little girl in front of her. And this dark mule is just as good for carrying packs, and the lady is to have him for her things and the little girl's." "Now," he continued, turning to me, "as soon as we stop, and have all had some dinner, you just pick out all the things you care most about, and put them by themselves; you can save out enough for two good sized packs; he's strong and he understands it, and we'll do them up snug for you, and show the men how to fasten them on safe; and you remember, now, that these two mules are yours till you get through to the gold-mines; and all Uncle Sam asks is that they shall be brought safely to his boys' headquarters in Sacramento City as soon as possible after you get into California."

Thus, by the wise forethought of our good Government, and the chivalrous management of this faithful agent, I was provided for to a sufficiency that would have looked to me, two hours before, like a fairy-dream. The programme for the afternoon was successfully carried out. Everything was arranged for an early morning start; and, at night, I lay down to sleep for the last time in the wagon that had proved such a shelter for months past. I remembered well how dreary it had seemed, on the first night of our journey (which now looked so long ago), to have *only* a *wagon* for shelter. Now we were not going to have even that. But, never mind, if we might only reach in safety the other foot of the mountains, all these privations would in their turn look small; and the same rich Providence that had led, and was still so kindly leading us, would, in that new land, perhaps, show us better things than we had seen yet. So, when morning came, I hailed it with cheerful hope, though with some misgivings, because I had not ridden horseback for several years, and, whenever I had, it had been with sidesaddle, and all the usual equipments for lady's riding, and, certainly, with no baby to carry. Now, I was to have only a common Spanish saddle, I must have Mary in front of me, and, it turned out, that several things needed for frequent use would have to be suspended from the pommel of my saddle, in a satchel on one side and a little pail on the other. At first I was rather awkward, and so afraid Mary would get hurt, that at uneven places in the road I would ask my husband to get up and take her, while I walked. But in a few hours this awkwardness wore off; and the second day of our new style of traveling I rode twenty five miles, only alighting once or twice for a brief time. Our friends, the government men, had left us the morning we left our wagon; taking the road to the Truckee where they felt themselves emphatically "due," considering their orders. I have more than once since wished I could see and thank them again; for, grateful as I felt then, I was able to appreciate more highly a thousand fold the service they had rendered us when, only ten days after we crossed the summit, the mountains were all blocked with snow, and the stormiest winter California had known for years was fully set in.

About the third day up the Carson, we were overtaken by a small company of men sent out on some special business which they did not state, from a western military station, and bound for California. Their animals were exclusively mules, and they were in every way fully equipped. They camped near us, and the commander, whom they called Col. J——., seemed much impressed with the defenselessness of our condition. Most of the young men shared this feeling more or less, and behaved very gentlemanly. Of course their animals could travel much faster than ours, so we could not hope to join their company. But Col. J——. suggested that as they had been traveling pretty fast for many days, and the ascent was now becoming more steep, it would be as well for them to make shorter days' rides till the summit was passed; in which case we might, by traveling a little later, camp near them at night, and so be less in danger from Indians. He said they would fire two or three guns when they stopped for the night, so that we might know they were within reach. This was indeed very acceptable aid; and we prized their company still more, when, on coming into camp the second night we found they had, during the afternoon, picked up a man whom they found by the road side, wounded by an Indian arrow. He had wandered off from his party a few days before, looking for game, had lost his way and had only that day regained the road. He was hurrying on alone, when an arrow from a thicket struck him and he fell. The supposition was that the Indians thought him dead, and were prevented from robbery, or further violence only by the sudden appearance of Col. J——.'s company. The wound was painful; but by the good care given him he gradually recovered.

On the 17th of October we reached the head of Carson Valley, and, just after noon, entered the great cañon. Here the road soon became so rough and steep as to make it very difficult for me to hold Mary and keep my seat. The men had hard work to drive the cattle and mules over the boulders at the frequent crossings of the stream, and in between the great masses of rock where the trail sometimes almost disappeared. As the cañon narrowed, the rocky walls towered, nearly perpendicular, hundreds of feet, and seemed in some places almost to meet above our heads. At some of the crossings it was well nigh impossible to keep the trail, so innumerable were the boulders, and the scraggy bushes so hid the coming-out place. The days were shortening fast, and, in this deep gulch, darkness began to come on early. The animals became more and more restive with the roughness of the way, and it was hard work to keep them from rushing into any narrow ravine that occasionally opened, or up some one of the steep trails which appeared now and then, suggesting unpleasant ideas of Indians and wild beasts. If our animals got many steps away we could not find them in the dusk. The young men had lagged behind most of the afternoon, leaving the driving mostly to the three of us, one of whom had to ride holding the child. Just as the shades were beginning to make everything look dim, we came to a crossing of the creek (which had now become a very small stream) where on the opposite side instead of the rocky walls we had had, there was a steep wooded hill up which wound a trail. But that could not be our way, for it was too steep; besides we had been told to keep the cañon, and we thought we could dimly trace *our* trail in the sand between the boulders, leading up stream. We paused to look closely; but the two mules with their large packs, one containing nearly all the food of the party, the other the most valuable goods we possessed, rushed resolutely forward up the creek bed, and disappeared among the brush. My husband, who had been carrying Mary for awhile, as I had become tired with the strain, hastily alighted, set her down on a flat rock, told me to take care of my mule for he must follow those animals; and quickly disappeared after them. At the same moment the men came up behind, which started the cattle forward and one of the oxen brushed close by Mary making her fall over into the water. In a moment I was there, had her in my arms, and found she was very little hurt, and her clothes but slightly wet. She was soon soothed; but meanwhile some of the cattle had rushed up the steep trail, and some had scattered among the bushes and boulders all eager to browse. Old Mr. A——. was trying to get together the latter, and young W——. was leading my mule to a convenient place for me to get on, when DeLu who had followed the cattle up the steep trail called out, "Come on, this is the way!" W——. and the old gentleman both questioned his correctness; but he insisted that the trail became plainer where he was; and when I said I could not ride up so steep a way in the dark, and hold Mary, he said, "O we'll come to an easier part pretty soon, you can get her up here afoot, and W——. can lead up the mule and then you can get on. Come, it's the only way." Thinking, from his positive tone, that he saw something we could not see, W——. and I followed, getting Mary along as well as we could. But, by the time we had climbed awhile, we found the steep growing steeper, and the trail almost disappeared. DeLu stopped, and the two or three cattle who had struggled up, began to tend downward again. It was evident we were lost in the cañon, and had better go no farther in the darkness. I sat down with Mary in my lap, wrapped her closely in my loose sacque [a full, hip-length jacket] and, feeling it a relief to rest instead of climb, soothed her and myself as well as I could; looked at the stars, was thankful there were no signs of a storm, and was conjecturing what had become of my husband and the mules, when the sound of a gun echoed through the cañon, followed soon by another; and we knew Col. J——.'s party were signaling us. The sound came from the direction in which the mules had disappeared; and so we hoped they and their driver had arrived at camp, and would soon send someone to guide us. We could only account for the lateness of the guns by supposing they had, like ourselves, met with some unusual adventure, or had forgotten. The young men now called down to old Mr. A——. to know if he had the other cattle. He told the number he had been able to get together, and, with those DeLu had, the whole number was complete. Slowly and with much slipping and sliding, DeLu now proceeded to get himself and the oxen down to the creek-bed once more. W——. led my mule in the same direction; and I followed with Mary, who instinctively clung close to my shoulder while I supported her with my left arm, and, with my right hand, took hold of bushes and branches to break the too rapid descent. I had not quite reached the bottom when a "Halloa!" was heard. We answered. From the darkness up the cañon help soon appeared, we were once more in line of march and, in less than an hour, arrived in camp.

The next day we climbed the first of the two ridges at the summit. And now I realized, in earnest, the value of a thoroughly trained mountain mule. In several places the way was so steep that the head of my animal was even with my eyes as I leaned forward with Mary's chief weight on my left arm while I clung with my right hand to the pommel of the saddle, obliged, for the time, to let the mule guide and drive himself. And nobly he did it, never slipping once; while the dark mule did as well with his great load. The other animals had to be driven, urged and kept in the track, while there seemed great danger of their packs being lost or torn; but, near evening, all arrived safely in camp. That night we slept within a few yards of snow, which lay in a ravine; and, water froze in our pans not very far from the fire; which, however, was rather low the last part of the night. But the morning was bright and sunny. "Hope sprang exultant"; for that day, that blessed 19th of October, we were to cross the highest ridge, view the "Promised Land," and begin our descent into warmth and safety. So, without flinching, I faced steeps still steeper than yesterday. I even laughed in my little one's upturned face, as she lay back against my arm, while I leaned forward almost to the neck of the mule, tugging up the hardest places. I had purposely hastened, that morning, to start ahead of the rest; and not far from noon, I was rewarded by coming out in advance of all the others, on a rocky height whence I looked, *down*, far over constantly-descending hills, to where a soft haze sent up a warm, rosy glow that seemed to me a smile of welcome; while beyond, occasional faint outlines of other mountains appeared; and I knew I was looking across the Sacramento Valley. California, land of sunny skies, that was my first look into your smiling face. I loved you from that moment, for you seemed to welcome me with loving look into rest and safety. However brave a face I might have put on most of the time, I knew my coward heart was yearning all the while for a home-nest and a welcome into it, and you seemed to promise me both.

A short time I had on those rocks, sacred to thanksgiving and prayer; then the others came, and boisterous shouts, and snatches of song made rocks and welkin [heaven] ring. We soon began to descend. Not far from the summit, on a small plateau, affording room to camp, and a little timber, we saw traces of fires, and, nearby, the carcasses of two fine horses evidently not very long dead; while a number of things scattered about looked like hasty flight. We concluded this must have been the scene of disaster of one of those unfortunate parties the relief men had told us of, who were caught in the two nights of snowstorm only about ten days before. And now very cheerily we found our way leading down, and down, and down, so suddenly in some places, that my mule braced his legs and slid. But the next day the descent was not so remarkable; the road became exceedingly dusty; and the spirits of the party flagged somewhat. We still, each night, made an effort to camp near Col. J——. and his men, for we had been warned that the Indians had in several instances attempted to attack and rob lone emigrants, while still high up in the mountains; though there would be no danger when we reached the mines. On the night of Oct. 21st we unloaded our packs and made our fires within a few rods of our courteous protectors. We had, as usual, made for our own little family a sort of barricade of packs somewhat retired from the others; the men were lying near their fire asleep; and all was still; when a sudden loud outcry, as of mingled pain and fright, followed by other hasty exclamations and rushing footsteps, and, soon, two or three shots, roused us all. We were quickly informed that two Indian arrows had been fired into our neighbors' camp, evidently aimed at the men who were sleeping in the light of their fire. One of the arrows had wounded a man, striking him directly on one of the large ribs, which had prevented its reaching the vitals. The other arrow missed its aim and fell on the ground. Several of the men rushed, armed, into the thicket whence the arrows came, fired, and pursued a short distance. But the enemy knew every turn better than strangers could, and no Indians were to be found. The wounded man proved not to be mortally wounded; and we had the satisfaction of knowing he was improving before we finally parted company, which occurred a day or two after. On the 24th of October at evening we reached what in our Guide Book was called "Pleasant Valley Gold Mines"; where we found two or three tents, and a few men with their gold-washing pans. They had been at work there for awhile; but said the little "diggings" just there were pretty much "worked out"; and they were going, in a day or two, over to Weaver Creek where, they told us, very fine "prospects had lately been struck," and there was quite a town growing up. That night, we slept, for the first time in several months, without the fear of Indians, or the dread of perils in advance. We rested ourselves and animals for two or three days, and then moved into the village of "Weaverville," of which the miners had told us. This village was made up of tents, many of them very irregularly placed; though in one part, following the trend of the principal ravine, there was, already, something like a row of these primitive dwellings, though at considerable distances apart. We added one to that row, and soon began to gather about us little comforts and conveniences, which made us feel as though we once more had a home. In a few days after we arrived in Weaverville, rain fell heavily, and soon the mountains just above us were blocked by snow. Only one company came through after us; and they barely escaped, by means of good mules.

But, with us, lovely sunny days followed the rainy nights; and, though the season, as a whole, was unusually stormy for California and doubtless would have been death to any caught at the mountaintops, yet there were intervals that seemed very delightful to those who had spent the preceding winter where the temperature ranged, for many weeks, below zero.

And now began my first experience in a California Mining Camp. The sense of safety that came from having arrived where there was no danger of attacks from Indians, or of perishing of want or of cold on the desert, or in the mountains, was at first so restful that I was willing, for awhile, to throw off anxiety; and, like a child fixing a play-house I sang as I arranged our few comforts in our tent. Indeed, part of the time it was fixing a play-house, for Mary was constantly pattering about at my side; and often, things were arranged for her convenience and amusement. Still, there was a lurking feeling of want of security from having only a cloth wall between us and out of doors. I had heard the sad story (which, while it shocked, reassured us) of the summary punishment inflicted in a neighboring town upon three thieves, who had been tried by a committee of citizens and, upon conviction, all hung. The circumstance had given to the place the name of Hang-Town. We were assured that, since then, no case of stealing had occurred in the northern mines; and I had seen, with my own eyes, buckskin purses half full of gold-dust, lying on a rock near the roadside, while the owners were working some distance off. So I was not afraid of robbery; but it seemed as if some impertinent person might so easily intrude, or hang about in a troublesome manner. But I soon found I had no reason to fear. Sitting in my tent sewing, I heard some men cutting wood up a hill behind us. One of them called out to another, "Look out not to let any sticks roll that way, there's a woman and child in that tent." "Aye, aye, we won't frighten them," was the reply, all spoken in pleasant, respectful tones. A number of miners passed every morning and afternoon to and from their work; but none of them stared obtrusively. One, I observed, looked at Mary with interest a time or two, but did not stop, till one day when I happened to be walking with her near the door, when he paused, bowed courteously and said, "Excuse me madam, may I speak to the little girl? We see so few ladies and children in California, and she is about the size of a little sister I left at home."[7] "Certainly," I said, leading her towards him. His gentle tones and pleasant words easily induced her to shake hands, and talk with him. He proved to be a young physician, who had not long commenced practice at home, when the news of gold discovery in California induced him to seek El Dorado, hoping thus to secure, more speedily, means of support for his widowed mother and the younger members of the family. His partner in work was a well-educated lawyer; and another of their party was a scientist who had been applying his knowledge of geology and mineralogy in exploring; and had lately returned from a few miles south with a report so favorable they intended in a day or two to go and make a claim on his newly discovered ground. Here, then, was a party of California Miners, dressed in the usual mining attire, and carrying pick, shovel and pans to and from their work, who yet were cultured gentlemen. I soon found that this was by no means a solitary instance. But a much larger number of the miners belonged to other very valuable classes of society. Merchants, mechanics, farmers were all there in large numbers. So that in almost every mining camp there was enough of the element of order to control, or very much influence, the opposite forces. These facts soon became apparent to me and, ere long, I felt as secure in my tent with the curtain tied in front, as I had formerly felt with locked and bolted doors. There was, of course, the other element as elsewhere; but they themselves knew that it was safer for law and order to govern; and, with a few desperate exceptions, were willing to let the lovers of order enjoy their rights and wield their influence. And the desperate exceptions were, for the time, so over-awed by the severe punishments some of their number had lately suffered, that, for a while, at least, in those early days, life and property were very safe in the mines; unless, indeed you chose to associate with gamblers and desperadoes; in which case, you of course constantly risked your money and your life. But, the same is true in the heart of New York, Philadelphia, or London. During my short residence, of only two months, in Weaverville I had but a few brief glimpses of the objectionable phases of society. Indeed, I ought not to say *glimpses*, for it was almost wholly through the ear, that anything of this kind came to me.

There was on the opposite side of the ravine, some rods down, a large tent, or rather, two tents irregularly joined, which, at first, I heard called a boarding house, then found was a public stopping place for travelers; and afterwards it turned out to include a full-fledged drinking and gambling saloon. From this place, at night, we sometimes heard the sound of loud talking; but I recollect only

once hearing anything alarming from there. That was past midnight, one rainy, dark night, when we were startled from sleep by
a loud shout, followed by various outcries, several running footsteps, and three or four pistol shots. We looked out and saw a light
or two in the direction of the saloon but heard no more of the
noise. The next morning we were told by one who had inquired
that a gambler who had lost several times, and saw himself about
to lose again, had snatched all the money from the table by a sudden movement and fled out into the darkness before anyone had
been aware of his intention. Then, two or three had followed with
shots; but he had escaped them. The other sound I caught from
that direction came through a woman, the only one besides myself
in the town. There had been another when I first came, a delicate
lovely invalid who, away back on the Platt River, had for awhile
traveled in the same company with us, riding much on horseback
in hope of benefiting her health. She and her husband staid in
Weaverville a short time but when the rains began they sought
the valleys farther to the south. This other woman who remained
was a plain person who, with her husband, had come from one
of the western states, and was acquainted only with country life.
She was probably between thirty and thirty five years of age, and
the idea of "shining in society" had evidently never dawned upon
her mind, when I first used to see her cooking by her out-door
camp fire, not far from our tent. Ordinary neighborly intercourse
had passed between us, but I had not seen her for some time,
when she called one day and in quite an exultant mood told me
the man who kept the boarding-house had offered her a hundred
dollars a month to cook three meals a day for his boarders, that
she was to do no dishwashing and was to have someone help her
all the time she was cooking. She had been filling the place some
days, and evidently felt that her prospect of making money was
very enviable. Her husband, also, was highly pleased that his wife
could earn so much.

Again I saw nothing of her for sometime, when again she
called, this time much changed in style. Her hair was dressed in
very youthful fashion; she wore a new gown with full trimmings,
and seemed to feel in every way elevated. She came to tell me there
was to be a ball at the public house in a few days; that several

ladies who lived at different camps within a few miles, chiefly at Hang-Town, were coming; and she came to say that I might expect an invitation as they would like very much to have me come. I laughingly declined, as being no dancer, and entirely unfitted to adorn any such scene. The assembly I think came off but I did not get even a glimpse of its glories; and as she, soon after, left the town, I never saw her again. I only remembered the circumstance because it amused me as being my first invitation into "Society" in California; and also, as it gave me a glimpse of the ease with which the homeliest, if not the oldest, might become a "belle" in those early days, if she only had the ambition, and was willing to accept the honor in the offered way.

Soon after arriving in Weaverville, my husband had met with an acquaintance who had been a traveling companion in the early part of our long journey. He had washed out a little gold, and was desirous to go into business. He had made two or three acquaintances who also thought this new mining settlement presented an opening for a store, but none of them were accustomed to trading. They understood that my husband was; so they proposed to him to enter into partnership with them, proceed immediately to Sacramento City to purchase goods, and they, by the time he returned, would have a place prepared to open a store. An effort was made to get a house built. The plan was to hew out timber for the frame, to split shakes for the roof and sides. But when they tried to get men to help them, so that the building could be done in anything like reasonable time, they found it impossible. All were so absorbed in washing out gold, or hunting for some to wash, that they could not think of doing anything else. On all sides the gold-pans were rattling, the cradles rocking, and the water splashing. So the best that could be done was to hew out some strong tent poles and ridges, and erect two good sized tents, one behind the other; the back one for dwelling, the front for a store. An opportunity occurred to buy a large cook stove, which was placed near the junction of the two tents. The back part of the back tent was curtained off for me, leaving a space round the cook stove for kitchen and dining room. One of the men slept in the store, and the other two had a small tent on one side. They managed to buy some packing boxes, and other odds and ends of lumber, and so made shelves and a counter, which did very well for those primitive times. We were soon fixed in our new quarters, the goods arrived from Sacramento, and business was opened. As one of the partners had formerly been in the meat business, some fat cattle were purchased, and beef was added to the other articles sold. This drew quite a crowd every morning; for fresh meat had not yet become very plentiful in the mines.

It had not been thought necessary for all the men of the firm to devote their time to the store. Two of them continued mining; so, when a large number of customers came together, I helped to serve them. This gave me an opportunity to see most of the dwellers in Weaverville and observe in a small way their behavior to each other. The majority of them were, as I have said, men of ordinary intelligence, evidently accustomed to life in an orderly community, where morality and religion bore sway. They very generally showed a consciousness of being somewhat the worse for a long, rough journey, in which they had lived semi barbarous lives, and for their continued separation from the amenities and refinements of home. Even in their intercourse with each other, they often alluded to this feeling, and in the presence of a woman, then so unusual, most of them showed it in a very marked manner. But, mingled with those better sort of men who formed the majority, were others of a different class. Roughly-reared frontier-men almost as ignorant of civilized life as savages. Reckless bravados, carrying their characters in their faces and demeanor, even when under the restraints imposed by policy. All these and more were represented in the crowd who used to come for their meat, and other provisions in the early morning hours. There were even some Indians, who were washing out gold in the neighboring ravines, and who used to come with the others to buy provisions. It was a motley assembly and they kept two or three of us very busy; for payments were made almost exclusively in gold-dust and it took longer to weigh that than it would have done to receive coin and give change. But coin was very rare in the mines at that time, so we had our little gold scales and weights, and I soon became quite expert in handling them. While thus busy, in near communication with all these characters, no rude word or impertinent behavior was ever offered me. But, among this moving crowd, thus working and eating, buying and selling, sounds of discontent and sadness were often heard. Discontent, for most of them had come to California with the hope of becoming easily and rapidly rich; and so, when they had to toil for days before finding gold, and, when they found it, had to work hard in order to wash out their "ounce-a-day"; and then discovered that the necessaries of life were so scarce it took much of their proceeds to pay their way,—they murmured and some of them cursed the country, calling it a "God forsaken land." While a larger number bitterly condemned their own folly in having left comfortable homes and moderate business chances for so many hardships and uncertainties. And still, many of them kept repeating this same folly, by being easily induced, when they had struck tolerably fair prospects, and were clearing twice as much per day as they had ever done before, to give up their present diggings and rush off after some new discovery, which was sure to be heralded every few days by the chronic "prospectors" who then (as too commonly ever since) kept the whole community in a ferment.

But the sounds of sadness were deeper and more distressing than those of mere discontent, for they were caused by sickness and death. Many ended their journey across the plains utterly prostrated by over exertion and too often poisoned by unwholesome food and want of cleanliness. Three or four young men living within a mile of us had crossed the country from the Missouri to the mines in three or four months; and during that whole time, as they reported to their neighbors, they had not once taken off any of their clothing—not even their boots—and had lived on salt meat and "hard-tack." Of course disease claimed them as natural prey. One of them died soon after arriving; the others suffered long; and, when we last heard of them, were still in a critical condition. But, aside from instances of glaring imprudence or ignorance, many felt the effects of long-continued over-exertion, extreme changes in temperature and ways of life, and, often, of sickening depression from the disappointment of too sanguine hopes. Those thus suffering were sad in voice and looks, needing all the cheering influence the healthful ones could afford. And many were the instances of brave, unselfish ministry among those often careless-appearing men.

But, spite of kind efforts, and attentions, there were, in our neighborhood, two or three cases of death and several of decided illness. My husband came home from a trip to Sacramento nearly prostrated by an attack of cholera-morbus, and was, some days, disabled from ordinary duties. Just as he had nearly recovered, a slow but powerful fever laid me helpless for a number of days. As soon as I was able to be moved, my bed was placed in a wagon, all the comforts and conveniences that could very well be carried in that way, were put in with me, a seat was fixed for Mary close by my side and, on the 27th of December, just two months from the time we entered Weaverville we set out for Sacramento City.

By the date, it was nearly midwinter, but by the little tufts of grass on the roadside, it was the beginning of spring; and as we descended the foot-hills, and struck the South Fork of the American River the season seemed to advance very rapidly. Flowers began to bloom in the turf, and early shrubs to blossom in the woods; while in the little thickets several species of birds flitted gayly about chirping and whistling their hints of the "good time coming." The genial atmosphere, bright sun and pleasant landscape assisted much in advancing my hitherto slow recovery. Appetite began to return, and the second evening of our journey, when we camped near a house where entertainment for travelers was offered, I asked the landlady to bake for me a sweet potato, a luxury which had lately been introduced into the mines from "The Islands." She did so, and we paid seventy five cents for it. They had no sleeping accommodations that were as comfortable as my bed in the wagon, so we had no occasion to acquaint ourselves with their terms for lodgings.

I have not thought it worthwhile to speak of prices in the mines, so much has been said on that subject in connection with every new mining settlement, but of course fresh meat was a half dollar per pound, butter a dollar, and other things in proportion. Yet we thought 75 cts for one baked sweet potato was quite equal to any charge we had heard of. However, when a few days afterwards in Sacramento City, one of our number paid a dollar for an onion and another twenty five cents for a quart of milk, and then saw the seller put water into the measure, we ceased to wonder at charges.

On the first day of January 1850 we arrived at Sutter's Fort; and I saw for the first time a spot of which I had heard and read away back in the Empire State, when, in laughing girlhood, I used to threaten I would go and see that Fort someday and stand on the Pacific shore; though I hardly expected then to do so. We paused for an hour's nooning where I could see, from my seat in the wagon, the old buildings, surrounded by the wall whose wide gate now stood open. As I looked, and thought of all I had read about "New Helvetia," the certainty of being really on the once far off Pacific coast became stronger. We rode on, and, before evening closed in, were camped in the City of Sacramento. There were more tents and cloth houses within sight than any other kinds of dwellings; and it was nothing strange to see a company living in a wagon; so we easily put up with that inconvenience for a day or two, till sufficient lumber was secured to lay a good floor, and over it was stretched a well made tent. In this our large cook-stove and several other newly-procured household conveniences were placed, and again we began housekeeping; though I was not yet able to sit up all day. The intention was to build a house as soon as possible, on this lot, which had been purchased before I came down, and here to open a general grocery and provision business. But the skies which had been so serene for a week or two, clouded over the day after we got into our tent, and the great rain of the season set in. Day after day it kept on, with only short intervals of such lovely sunshine as we had never before seen in January. I, of course, could not go out a step to see anything, only stand at times in the doorway, when the sun broke out, looking at the soft green turf and the grandly broken clouds for a few minutes; then all would be shadow again, and rain, rain, rain would pour down for hours. Two of the partners in the mines had come with my husband, and were impatient to build and open [a] business, but at present nothing could be done but attend to the cattle part of the time every day. As they went and came I could hear from my curtained corner, where in my weakness I had to spend much of my time, the news of the neighborhood, and various discussions as to the probabilities of business, the weather, etc. In a day or two they began to talk about the rise of the river, or rather, the rivers, for both the Sacramento and American, I learned, began to look threatening; especially the latter, whose banks were very low just back of the City, where the old settlers said, it had more than once overflowed and filled "the sloo" sometimes spreading farther.[8] Speculations about the danger were various; but, on the whole, the hope seemed to prevail that "the sloo" being lower than the ground where most of the city was located, would make a channel for the superfluous waters and let them flow away across the flats to mingle again with the Sacramento some miles below. So, though I knew there was danger, I did not dwell very anxiously upon it; but used every effort to recover strength. On the evening of the 9th of January, I had put Mary quietly to bed and was resting myself for a minute or two before undressing for the night, when I heard quick footsteps without, and Mr. A——.'s voice saying hastily to my husband who stood at the door, "The water's coming in." The reply expressed doubt; but A——.'s voice continued very emphatically, "O, yes, I am sure,—I have just been to the 'sloo,' and the water is flowing over the banks fast. See, come this way, to this low spot, and you will soon find yourself stepping in water. There, watch a minute, don't you see it rising on your boot?" A prompt assent was the reply, and I heard them in a few hasty words agree upon what was to be done. One of the few good houses within sight was the residence of a Dr. M——. and wife. He had come early to the country as an army surgeon, had quickly accumulated wealth, sent for his wife, and made a home in this fast growing city, where he owned several blocks of land. About a hundred yards from our tent he had lately built a story-and-a-half double house intending it for rent in two tenements. It was not finished, but was inclosed and roofed, and two stairways were built, one in each end of the house, leading to the upper rooms. In the hurried words I heard between A——. and my husband, it was agreed that A——. should go to Dr. M——.'s house and ask permission for us to take possession of one of those upper rooms; while my husband should prepare Mary and me for a hasty removal. While they were thus talking outside I had risen from my languid position, put on my rubbers and cloak, and had Mary in my arms dressing her when my husband came in. He saw that I had heard their conversation, and no explanations were necessary, so he went rapidly to work rolling up bed and bedding. I did what I could to help in gathering together and putting into portable shape some of the conveniences most immediately needed, and which it was most essential to keep dry; and by the time A———. returned with permission for us to take possession of the desired room, we had several things ready to be removed. Meantime, the water was filling up all the depressions, and, when we stepped out into the darkness, we soon found we must hasten or it would be over shoe-tops. However, I managed with help, to reach one of the front doors of the house, ascend the stairs and sit down on one of the bundles already there with Mary safe beside me, ere the water had entirely covered the ground. Then sitting still there, I could hear the rippling and gurgling as it rose higher and began to find its way into crevices and over sills in the lower story. It was evidently rising very fast. The men kept coming and going between the tent and house, carrying such things as could be carried in the arms, and brought directly upstairs. But, even by the second time they returned, the water was up to their ankles and it was not long before they were obliged to cease, and abandon to the flood all that remained.

By this time others had taken refuge in our little ark. A bed had been made in a corner and blankets tacked up for a partition, and there Mary and I took refuge; while the men gathered round a stove that had been left there by some of the workmen who had boarded themselves while building. We could tell by the sounds through the partition-wall that a much larger number of persons had gathered in the other end of the house. Voices of all tones were heard there, from the stalwart bass to the shrill cry of infancy. We heard, the next day, that, by midnight, fifty persons had taken refuge in that part of the house, among them Mrs. Dr. M———. herself. Her home was on rather higher ground, and, though but one story in height, was, for an hour or two, considered safe; but at last it became evident that the flood would soon cover the floors. Then, abandoning all but a few of the most necessary things, she was conveyed in a friendly boat to the little room where soon so many others had already flocked. From the time we had found ourselves safe above the waters, the thought of the hundreds who must be exposed to the same dangers, and the wonder what could become of them, had been very distressing to me. But, as the first confusion subsided, and I found refuge in my curtained corner, I discovered, by the regular strokes of oars which every now and then passed near the house, and the voices mingled with them, that help was being very busily and efficiently rendered. I heard occasionally the words of some who came in boats and climbed into the windows of the house. Then, inquiries would be called out to others passing by and answers given, by all of which I found that the boats of all the vessels lying in the river had been promptly manned and set in motion as soon as needed; that many other boats owned in the neighborhood were being freely used, and that thus far, all who had been found in danger had been rescued. Hundreds had flocked and were flocking to "the ridge," a strip of high land, well above the water, a mile or two east of where we were; many had been taken on board vessels in the river, and so, it seemed, thus far, all had been in some way provided for. This was very cheering, and as soon as the various voices and other sounds became quiet, welcome sleep came to our relief. In the morning boats were again heard close to the house, and I soon found out that most of those in the other part of the house were being conveyed away, either to go to San Francisco, or to the high ground back of the town. All, in our end, except our own little party, also left, and as soon as I felt able, I managed to get dressed and go to the window. For miles north and south I could see nothing but water, bearing upon its surface boats and various odd looking craft. Eastward the expanse of water was narrower, and, beyond it, was the ridge which looked, in the distance, much like an enormous Mississippi raft, covered with a dense mass of moving creatures of some kind, though it was impossible for the eyes at our distance to distinguish them one from the other. Soon some acquaintances of A——. and H——. came near in a boat and they let themselves down from the window into the little craft and went toward the ridge to see if they could get some fresh meat. They had previously been told by some passers-by that provisions had been removed from the stores the night before and conveyed to the ridge in quantities sufficient to prevent a famine till more could come from San Francisco; and fresh beef was being brought from the neighboring country. In due time they returned with such supplies, as, added to what had been saved the night before, secured us enough to live on for a few

days. Sufficient stove wood had been hurried upstairs among the
first things the night before to cook several meals. Thus we were
saved from danger of want for the present. The men had arranged
with their friends who had boats to call at the window occasionally so that we might be sure of opportunities of communication
with the "land beyond the flood," and also with the vessels on the
river; for, already, the plan of going to San Francisco by the next
steamer that could be taken was under discussion. But for nearly
a week there was no opportunity of getting down to the Bay
without such inconveniences and risks as seemed worse than our
present position. There were at that time but two steamers running on the Sacramento, neither of them very fast, one, extremely
slow. One had started down, the morning after the flood set in,
so crowded with passengers and goods that there was neither
safety nor comfort on board. The other was expected up in a day
or two; but for some reason was delayed. Other vessels were taking passengers down, but were most of them too heavily loaded
to be safe. So, for a number of days, Mary and I were absolutely
imprisoned by the waters. The only outlook from our end of the
house was toward the Ridge, and to the North and South. We
could not look toward the River at all, and so had not the variety
of seeing vessels arriving or departing. As the men went and came
they brought accounts by no means cheering of the condition of
things on the Ridge. Many had escaped thither with very little to
shield them from suffering or save them from want. Yet, those
who had health, most of them managed to work bravely, and
keep up hope. But there were sick ones there, poorly sheltered,
and cared for but slightly. In two or three instances our men saw
the dying and heard them ask for friends to pray with them. In
one or two places the dead lay stretched out ready for burial.
But, worse still, the reckless and heartless were there, in some
instances making the air ring with their discordant mirth, while
they carried on their gambling and drinking. There were accounts
too, of some shameful instances of extortion which occurred the
first night of the flood; in one of which it was said, a boatman
refused to take on board a man who was clinging to the ridge of
a small tent, almost submerged, until the latter should pay twenty
dollars; which he declared he could not do, having lost all his

money. The brutal fellow was about to row off, leaving the nearly drowned man to perish, when a heavily laden ship's boat came up. The Captain divined the difficulty at once, and under cover of a pistol compelled the first boatman to take aboard the suffering man and row along-side the larger boat to a place of safety; assuring him that if he attempted to disobey orders he should be shot instantly. Such cases showed that there were about us desperately selfish men, who would stop at nothing for the sake of gain; but I am glad to say we heard of few such things; while instances of generous aid and ready sympathy were common.

While we were thus water-bound, in a very ordinary, unfinished frame house, the water in the lower story reaching not far from half-way up to the rafters of our floor, there came a night of strong wind, rising, toward midnight, to a heavy gale. Sweeping over so many miles of water, it was not long in raising quite a sea. The waves dashed against the sides of the house, shaking and rocking it so that there seemed great danger of its capsizing. The noise of wind and waves made sleep, for some hours, impossible to me; and as I lay there in the darkness I tried to prepare myself to seize Mary and cling to whatever might be uppermost, in case the house careened. But, through this danger also, we were mercifully preserved and, in a day or two afterward, the old steamer "McKim" was announced in port, and I was told to be ready to depart on the morrow.

On the morning of the 15th of January a pretty good sized boat was moored under the window; Mary was handed down, and then, by means of a ladder firmly steadied, I descended safely, and we were afloat. As we neared the river-channel, we saw many more buildings than were visible in our late neighborhood, and presently we were riding down the middle of a street with houses on each side, some, dwellings only, then stores with dwellings attached, then warehouses, one or two hotels, etc; all submerged up to about half the height of the first story. Most of them were, for the time, forsaken; though, in some cases, men were busy in boats, fishing out various things from the ground floors, and placing them up above; or carrying them away to safer places. We had little difficulty in getting on board the steamer, and, after some delay set off, but did not arrive in San Francisco till the next morning. Dreary were the sights on each side, as we steamed slowly down the stream. For miles nothing but muddy water, with here and there trees and shrubs, sometimes singly, sometimes in clusters and groves, rising above the surface. Occasionally there was a mound or a ridge, reaching above the water; and, upon it, a group of cattle huddled shivering together. Shivering, not because the weather was cold, but because they were more or less wet, and had eaten but little for days. Sometimes there was a cabin or shanty on the rise, and one or two human forms could be seen. Once, and I think only once, a woman and a child or two were seen with the men; and, very rarely, a stack of hay gave signs of forethought, and made one feel like shouting congratulations to the happy animals surrounding it. But that was a very unusual sight in those days, and has been too much so in many of the years since. The morning of the 16th was a little cloudy at first, but soon brightened, and when I came on deck, I found we were anchored in the Bay of San Francisco, at some distance from the shore. Directly in front of us was Telegraph Hill, and very cheery did it look to me, after all the dreary scenes of the past few days, with its sides, not then torn and disfigured as they are now, but clothed with bright verdure, and bathed in warm sunlight. The old, red building on its summit looked quaint and interesting with a bright-colored flag floating above it. It became an object of still greater interest, when I was told it stood there as signal-bearer keeping up communication between vessels outside the Golden Gate and men in the heart of San Francisco.

It seemed that our Steamer could not safely approach any nearer the shore; so the unloading of freight and passengers was effected by means of lighters. It was nearly noon when we landed on one of the wharves. I had to sit for awhile in a warehouse office, while my husband went to inquire for rooms where we might put up. After some time he returned looking rather puzzled. He said he had not been able to hear of a place where rooms, or even one room, could be got; but there was a public house not far off, where we could get dinner; and probably Mary and I could sit there for an hour or two, while he and Mr. A——. looked farther for rooms or a house. Accordingly we walked, with not very elastic footsteps, to The Montgomery House, which Mr. A——. said they had been informed was the best, if not the only, Hotel to be found within easy distance. It fronted on Montgomery St. not very far from Commercial. The building was long in proportion to its width, its framework was frail, and was covered on the outside partly with boards, and partly with canvas, diversified, if I recollect rightly with sheets of zinc, in places that particularly needed staying, or, had proved extra leaky. The inside was partly lined with cloth. The front door was in the middle of the gable end and was reached by two or three rough board steps from the decidedly muddy footpath which, then and there, was the side-walk of Montgomery St. As we entered we were motioned to the right, where was a small room wholly without carpet, contain-ing one table, and a very few chairs, and lighted by one window. This was the sitting room. The partition which separated it from the dining room behind it was of cloth. Across the little hall-way into which the front door opened, and directly opposite the sit-ting room door, was the bar-room, a much larger apartment than the sitting-room, and furnished with a box-stove, the only place for a fire in the whole house, excepting the cook stove in the kitchen; which latter apartment was behind the bar-room. From the little hall-way, and facing the front door ascended a flight of stairs. At the top of these you found yourself in a hall extending the whole length of the building, and of just sufficient width to allow a passage by the side of the stairway to the front end. The partitions on each side were wholly cloth, and, at distances of about four feet apart along the whole length of the hall, on both sides, were narrow doorways. Looking into one of these door-ways, you saw before you a space about two and a half feet wide and six feet long, at the farther end of which was a shelf or stand on which you could place a candlestick, while you had just room to stand and dress or undress. At the side of this space were two berths, one above the other; and these berths, so situated, were the only sleeping accommodations afforded by this Hotel. Of course when I entered the house I had not the least idea of ever knowing anything about its sleeping accommodations. I sup-posed that in two or three hours, I should be in a private room, resting, preparatory to arranging a home nest. But when, after spending the afternoon searching, both the seekers returned and said nothing of the kind we wanted could be found, there was no alternative but to remain where we were.

The landlord thoughtfully proposed to the two lodgers who occupied the berths at the farther end of the hall, against the wall of the house, to give them up to us; thus placing us in the most private spot to be obtained; for which I certainly felt grateful. The next morning efforts to obtain a place to live were renewed, with similar results. An opportunity was offered of renting a whole house, which would be vacated in a few days by a family going to the mines; but it was three times as large as we needed; besides being too lonely a place for me to be left alone in, while business was attended to.

Meantime, with all the discomforts of these surroundings, health was returning to me, and I was able to walk out a little with Mary. I could not go far from the door, at least in one direction, without coming pretty nearly in contact with a fact the mention of which has since been so common with old Californians, when speaking of early San Francisco days, that any allusion to it has now become the signal for a broad smile with those who have had frequent interviews with Pioneers. I understand there is a gentleman in San Francisco, deeply interested in California history, who holds it to be a serious indication of spurious pretenses, if any one claiming to be an early Pioneer does not, within five minutes after beginning to talk about those old times, say that he has "seen the time when tide water came up to Montgomery St." I hasten, therefore, to say that "I saw tide water come up to Montgomery St.," and, more, that it was on one occasion with difficulty I avoided stepping into it, within a very short distance of the door of our Hotel. However, by turning to the right from the door, and going up a street which was then very steep, one soon got away from the water, and up to where there was a fine view of the Bay and the shores beyond. Up this hill I managed slowly to walk and lead Mary and very greatly did we both enjoy the warm sunshine, soft breeze and sparkling scene. Turning in a fresh direction, we came to where there were a number of odd looking shanties, several of them displaying in doors and windows strangely-shaped packages, many-colored boxes and, in some places, queer toys. It took me but a minute or two to see that the people who stood in these doors, or walked busily about, were Chinese. I had seen but one or two since coming into San Francisco, and, before that, the only Chinese I had ever seen was one who in my youth was brought by Missionaries to America and visited an Eastern city where I lived. This little nucleus of the since celebrated China-Town of San Francisco was to me, that January morning in 1850, an unexpected sight; and I was for a few minutes as much amused as Mary; but the outlandish look of everything soon made me feel out of place; and I was hastening to find a street I could turn down, when an elderly Chinaman with a long cue and blue cloth sack came from a store door, with smiling face, addressed to me a word or two of salutation in broken English, then stooped down, shook hands with Mary and placed in her hand a curious Chinese toy. I tried to decline it, but he insisted upon her keeping it, and she was so much pleased, I thanked him and inquired the price. He positively declined taking pay for it, so Mary received her first present in San Francisco from a Chinaman.

Now came a rainy day or two, greatly magnifying all the disagreeable features of our surroundings. Everybody boarding at our Hotel was now obliged to keep within doors; and those not engaged in regular business had to spend the whole day crowded into the little comfortless sitting room or huddled, as they could get chances, around the bar-room stove. There was necessarily much confusion; there were of course many there who were far from refined in manners; yet, I must say in all candor, that during those three very unpleasant days, I received no rough or discourteous word from anybody; I witnessed no offensive behavior; and, whatever there was of drinking at the bar, I saw no drunkards, either at the bar-room stove or in the sitting room. I was repeatedly very kindly invited to a warm seat at the stove with Mary; and never went there without finding room cheerfully made. But we could not live in this way long. Efforts were being made, but no place for us had yet been found. At last, on Saturday morning of this tedious week a new face appeared upon the scene, introduced by Mr. A——. It was the Rev. Mr. W——. Pastor of a Protestant Church, organized in San Francisco but a few months before. He had heard that a family were staying at the Montgomery House who wished to get rooms for housekeeping; and he came to give information and make a suggestion which he thought would be a relief. He said a friend of his had just built a house on purpose to rent in tenements. Only one tenement was yet finished and that one Mr. W——. was occupying with his small family; but another would soon be finished, which he thought we might get. Meantime, there was one room, besides his own apartments, which was habitable. We could no doubt secure that immediately, and we could board in his family until a place was ready for us to keep house.

We were not long in availing ourselves of this hospitable offer, and before night we were safely sheltered, and our little comforts piled about us, in a room which, though unfinished, was more comfortable than any place we had occupied for many months.

The conveniences of civilized life, the comforts of home, can not be keenly appreciated, or even fully seen, by those who have never been, for a time, shut out from them. Repeatedly in the days that now followed, did I find myself feeling that I had never before known the brightness of the evening lamp-light nor the cheeriness of the morning breakfast room, with all their orderly accompaniments; that I had never before realized the worth of quiet domestic life, unworried by ever-threatening dangers. Still more impressive were the new emotions felt the first time I attended Church in California. The building was larger than I had expected; and I soon saw the reason; for the numbers that gathered promptly, and seated themselves without hesitation, showed that a large congregation was the ordinary rule. On each side of the speaker's platform, which extended well forward, the seats were arranged sidewise, and those nearest the wall continued in that position some distance; so that, seated as I was near the centre of the house, facing the pulpit, I had a nearly full view of a good many faces. There were very few women; not more, I think, than six or eight in the whole assembly. They were dressed with the unassuming neatness common among Christian ladies at the east, their manner was quiet, self-possessed and devout, and they were treated by the gentlemen with the courtesy always expected among Americans, which of course, restrained every indication of marked notice. Yet one could not help seeing, in most of the masculine faces, expressions of high appreciation and profound deference, as, by one's and two's, the few women entered and took their seats. A small choir occupied a low platform behind the congregation and, with their very good voices and correct time, led the plain familiar tunes; almost every one present joining heartily in the singing. Toward the close of the service a good anthem was well given by the choir. During prayer, quietness, reverence, devotion pervaded the assembly. When the speaker had announced his text and made one or two introductory remarks, the motionless quiet which prevailed drew my attention, and my eyes wandered to the mass of faces on each side the desk. Never before had I realized the sublimity of the human countenance. They were nearly all men, in youth or in the prime of life. Every one was listening with fixed attention. There was an intensity of earnestness; a glow of intelligence in every face that made me involuntarily bow my head, and thank God for making so grand a being as man, and for letting me once more look upon so large a number, thus exercising the highest functions of intelligent beings, worshipping; adoring; and reverently receiving instruction from their Divine Creator. Whether the experiences through which those men had passed in the months just gone by, had taught them meanings in life, and power in spiritual truth they had never known before, thus illumining their faces, or whether I was favored that day in seeing an assemblage of exceptionally good men, I will not say; but such were my impressions of the first worshipping congregation I ever saw in California.

Two months from the time we left the Montgomery House we began housekeeping in one of the tenements for which we had been waiting. The whole building was now completed, and being, for those early days, conveniently arranged and neatly finished, though with cloth and paper only, it was soon occupied by a number of the most respectable and companionable people in San Francisco. The owner himself established a boarding house in one part of it, and the other tenements were taken, in some cases by those who wished to board with him, in others by those who, like ourselves, kept house. Nearly all were from the eastern or the middle states, a very few were from the south. Most of them were Church-going people. Some of them came to the house immediately on their first arrival in California, others had been in the city a number of months; but nearly all of them had some acquaintances in other parts of the town; and, as much sociability and kindly feeling prevailed, there was opportunity for the inmates of the house to get a fair insight into social life in San Francisco at that time. Much has been said on this subject and many dark pictures have been drawn. No doubt those dark pictures were true to life, in individual instances far too numerous; but just beside them, within the walls of neighboring dwellings, sometimes under the same roof, might have been drawn pictures as true of social circles in which refinement, morality, and religion were fondly cherished, and as faithfully illustrated in domestic life, as in homes on the Atlantic shore.

Any newcomer into San Francisco in those days had but to seek, in the right way, for good people and he could find them. But in the immense crowds flocking hither from all parts of the world there were many of the worst classes, bent upon getting gold at all hazards, and if possible without work. These were constantly lying in wait, as tempters of the weak. A still greater number came with gold-getting for their ruling motive, yet intending to get it honestly, by labor or legitimate business. They did not at all intend, at first, to sacrifice their habits of morality, or their religious convictions. But many of them bore those habits and held those convictions too lightly; and as they came to feel the force of unwonted excitement and the pressure of unexpected temptation, they too often yielded, little by little, till they found themselves standing upon a very low plain, side by side with those whose society they once would have avoided. It was very common to hear people who had started on this downward moral grade, deprecating the very acts they were committing, or the practices they were countenancing, and concluding their weak lament by saying, "But *here* in California we *have* to do such things." Never was there a better opportunity for demonstrating the power and truth of Christian principle than was, in those days, open to every faithful soul; and, never perhaps were there in modern civilized society more specious temptations to laxity of conduct. And thus it came to pass that in this our early California life, while we had the pleasures of associating with those who were true to their convictions, earnest in their religious life, and faithful and lovely in the domestic circle; yet, on the other hand, we often met people who had let loose the reins of moral government over themselves and families; and consented that others should do so.

A house constructed and occupied as was the one where we lived, which I have described, was a little world in itself; containing specimens of various types of character; and covering under its roof many phases of life. During the thirteen months we spent there, two little girls were born in the house into two different families; one death occurred, that of a man in the prime of life, for many years a sea captain; and one wedding was solemnized and celebrated with considerable hilarity. Thus was completed within that small space the cycle of human events. But we who dwelt there were connected with many others outside, and so were in contact with the life in general of the city and the state. We saw the beginnings of that system of "street grading" which has since so transformed the face of the site of San Francisco. We gazed with terror on the awful fire of May 4th 1850. We witnessed the erection of new churches, and the inauguration of religious news-papers. As the year advanced we experienced the alarm of approaching cholera. We lived through the days when it paced slowly, hither and thither in the city; striking down one here and another there; but never raging as an epidemic. While, at the same time, we were hearing daily of its fearful ravages in Sacramento City, the only place in California where it has ever prevailed alarmingly, and that year the only time. In the early fall of 1850 we were all excitement to hear the result of California's knock at the door of the Union; and as the day approached when the Steamer would bring the decision, many eyes were strained toward Telegraph Hill. At length the signal went up;—the Oregon was outside the heads and would soon be in the harbor. As she neared, another signal indicated that she carried flying colors, implying good news, and presently she appeared in sight of those who like ourselves overlooked North Beach; gay with streamers, and flags of all nations,—the Stars and Stripes most prominent, and, above them, straightened out by the generous wind which seemed to blow a long breath on purpose, floated the longest streamer of all, displaying the words "California Admitted!" The roar of cannon rolled over the waters, and met answering roars from Fort and ships. Everybody was laughing. "Now we are at home again!" cried one. "Yes," was the answer, "and remember, all, we must no more talk of going to 'The States' nor hearing from 'The States.' We are *in* 'The States!'"

Well do I remember the brisk tap at my door that morning and the friendly voice that invited me up to a high veranda to take a look, through a large Field Glass, at the welcome Steam Ship. For some minutes we stood there looking in silence; the sight brought thoughts too many and too absorbing for words. Then, with brief expressions of thanksgiving and mutual congratulation, we descended, meeting and answering, as we passed through the halls and porches, the laughing congratulations of our fellow-inmates.

This was in October of 1850. But during the Spring and Summer of that year, the business marts of San Francisco were the scenes of speculations, of venturesome investments, of reverses and successes, which, to record, would take volumes; and the effects of which still live, for good or ill, in the lives of hundreds of Californians. It is sometimes said that all the old Pioneers are poor men. Doubtless this is too sweeping. Quite a number of those Pioneers laid the foundation, even in those early days of extravagant undertakings, for permanent business, and substantial prosperity. With clear heads, steady nerves and conscientious principles, they persevered in whatever line of business they had undertaken, and thus secured for themselves, in some cases great wealth, in more a competence, and are now among the pillars of Californian society; with well educated families grown up about them, who, in their turn, are rearing children to follow in the good paths of their grand-sires.

But the temptations to rash speculation were, in those days, very great; and there were men who came here from broken-down enterprises in the east, chafed nearly to desperation and determined to make almost any venture to recover themselves. Others came comparatively inexperienced, but with inflated ideas of their own business-capacities, and of the opportunities this new business-world would surely open to them. Here and there was an individual in whom all the conditions just named met, and that man was bound to make a desperate dash, and as certainly bound to fail, and, alas, almost as certainly bound to repeat the same experience every three or five years since, till, "the old Californian *is* a poor man."

One of the above-described characters boarded a vessel just arrived in port and lying out in the stream freighted with potatoes and onions. It was early in 1850. Vegetables of all kinds were very scarce. Potatoes and onions were specially in demand. He had been watching for some to arrive; and having seen a notice of this ship, pushed out at morning's dawn to seize the prize. He was ahead of everybody, succeeded in securing the purchase, left the Captain's office, and, before he reached the edge of the deck, he met another man coming on the same errand. The late comer made him an offer for his bargain by accepting which he could have cleared, at once, about nine hundred dollars. But he promptly refused. He had not enough money to close the purchase himself, but he borrowed some, got the potatoes and onions, rented a small place near the upper end of Long Wharf, and began business. The man through whom he borrowed the money, seeing the promising prospect, proposed to go in with him, introducing at about the same time two or three other acquaintances who had *some* money, and who, he said, were ready to join the enterprise when any thing offered too large for the first two to manage.

Very soon other cargos came in. They said they must buy all the potatoes that arrived so as to keep control of the market. The two or three who were ready to "put in" some money, were very quickly "in" so deeply that they had to borrow money of others farther outside. For awhile they sold rapidly and well, and the two who kept the store might be seen going home every afternoon, each with a heavy pouch under one arm, while, between them, hung upon a stout stick they carried a wooden bucket, so nearly full of coin that the strong iron bail was bent almost to an angle. At first they bought onions at fifty cents per pound, and sold some for a dollar, some for seventy five cents. Potatoes purchased for 20 and 22 cts were sold for from 30 to 40 cts. But of course if, as was the case, new supplies kept coming, these prices could not continue. Soon a large ship entered the harbor claiming to have on board seventy five tons of potatoes. "The Firm" was getting desperate. Without examination of the condition of the cargo, they purchased at 25 cts per pound and committed themselves in such a way that they could not draw back without fear of legal troubles. As soon as they began to unload it was found that the potatoes had been stowed into the ship in small manilla sacks, which now, most of them, burst as soon as laid hold of, thus scattering the contents over the whole deck of the vessel. They had to be shoveled, or in any way thrown, from the deck into the lighter, and from the lighter on to the wharf. There they were scattered from the end of Long Wharf to the store, while "wharf rats," both bipeds and quadrupeds, as well as some bipeds that were *not* wharf rats, were free to help themselves. When the purchasers complained to the Captain, of whom they had bought, pleading that the cargo was not in marketable order, he flew into a passion and threatened to shoot or throw overboard anybody that tried to make him trouble. So they went on unloading, paying enormous sums for help, which, in many cases, they were obliged to hire at a dollar per hour, so scarce was labor at that time. Still, more potatoes kept arriving. Two men of the firm were sent to Sacramento City to sell, and many tons were shipped to them. Another went for the same purpose to Stocton. The latter sold pretty steadily, but not very rapidly nor profitably. The Sacramento men did not remit. Somebody went to see about it. One of them had settled himself near the wharf with potatoes by tons piled all about him, refusing to sell because prices were not high enough he said; the other had taken some of the money he handled, and had invested it in a gambling enterprise. While the partner who had gone to investigate the difficulties in Sacramento was busy trying to straighten the crooked doings there, new arrivals of potatoes were announced almost daily in San Francisco. The acting partner left in the store fretted and fumed, and wished the port could be closed. He wanted to keep on borrowing money to buy up all the new arrivals; which of course might then be purchased at much lower rates; but he refused to sell on the falling market, though that was now the only course left open to them.

It is useless to prolong the story. The crash and the ruin soon came. There were criminations and recriminations; there was one lawsuit, and others were threatened. But nothing could arrest or neutralize the natural results of reckless speculation, extravagant expansion, and bad management. It was not alone in the cities, and in ordinary commerce that these wild things were done. Men entered into contracts to buy herds of cattle, intending to turn them into beef to supply the San Francisco market; and found on starting into the enterprise that catching the cattle, and getting them to where they could be handled, required more men and horses than they could get; besides involving other enormous expenses which they had not taken into account. In other cases large tracts of land were purchased with the intention of making them cattle ranges or of cutting hay. But the purchase being chiefly on credit, or with borrowed money, and the returns being long in coming, interest ate up the purchaser, and often involved him hopelessly. In the mines, it soon became an admitted adage that "mining was a lottery"; but it was not more so, than such business enterprises as these.

In the social life of San Francisco, one of the sensations of that year was an entertainment got up for the benefit of a Benevolent Society which, even in that early day, had been organized months before, and had done, and continued doing, works of mercy, which cheered and saved many a lonely wanderer. The entertainment was conducted by the Ladies of the different Churches, of which there were, in the city, already four. Everything went prosperously on the day of the festival, and in the evening a large crowd gathered for social enjoyment. Introductions and cordial greetings were turning strangers into friends and making many, hitherto lonely, hearts feel that even in California there was society worth having, when there entered the room a man, prominent for wealth and business-power, bearing upon his arm a splendidly-dressed woman, well known in the city as the disreputable companion of her wealthy escort. With cool assurance he proceeded to make her and himself quite at home; but in a few minutes he was waited upon by a committee of gentlemen, who called him aside and told him they were sent by the lady-managers to say that they declined to receive as an associate, or to have introduced to their daughters, one who stood in the relation occupied by his companion, and they respectfully requested him to invite her to withdraw with him. Of course there was nothing for him to do but to comply; and all went on again pleasantly. It was reported that he had previously boasted that he could introduce "Irene" *anywhere* in San Francisco; but the events of that evening proved to him, as well as to others, that while Christian women would forego ease, and endure much labor, in order to benefit any who suffered, they would not welcome into friendly association any who trampled upon institutions which lie at the foundation of morality and civilization.[9]

But, while this lofty and decided stand was taken upon these important points by the wise, and was approved even by the less judicious, there were some habits gaining ground among the thoughtless and selfish which gave me uneasiness; and which I could not help feeling presaged evil for the future. One of these was the custom, early begun, of gentlemen manifesting their gallantry by expensive presents to their lady acquaintances. This seemed to be done at first in a sort of off-handed, jocular way, probably without much thought as to its motives or results. There were but few ladies. It was natural there should be a little feeling of rivalry among the gentlemen in competing for the favor of those few. Money, while it was easily lost, was, in those days, often as easily won. When a gentleman of social disposition "made a strike," as they commonly expressed it, he often liked to tell his lady friends in a laughing way of his good management or unexpected luck. An easy way to introduce the subject was to jokingly toss at her, or in some way offer, a pretty present; and tell her it was a treat on the strength of "so and so." There were, I am glad to say, ladies of such dignity of character and self-respect as to prevent, without direct effort, any such advances; but there were too many whose cupidity and vanity were stronger than delicacy of feeling or sense of propriety; and I blushed to discover, by conversations held in my presence, that there were instances of women watching each other jealously, each afraid the other would get more or richer presents than herself. This evil became painfully prominent, as time went on and more families came to the coast, in connection with musical and literary entertainments, school-exhibitions, etc. Little girls and young ladies who sung, played or recited on such occasions often received, thrown at their feet before they left the stage, expensive jewelry, or even pieces of coin. They commonly accepted them; often with looks of exultation; and, still worse, there were mothers, who not merely countenanced the thing, but even boasted of the amount their daughters had thus received. It must indeed be an obtuse moral sense that could not perceive the corrupting tendency of such customs; and I have since seen some sad falls into positive vice of those whose downward course appeared to begin in these and similar practices.

For nearly three years after our first arrival in San Francisco, we lived on the borders of the Bay. Less than half the time was spent in the City, the remainder, nearly all, in one of the most beautifully located villages that the Steamboat traveler of those early days admired, as he journied from the Metropolis to the interior. During those two or three years there first came under my observation some of the unfavorable effects of the great California emigration movement upon American domestic life. The first case which called my attention to the subject was that of an acquaintance whom we had met on the plains, and who had ever since continued, at short intervals, to turn up somewhere in our vicinity, wherever it might be. He had from the beginning of our acquaintance been very free in telling about his wife and family, in an off-handed common-place way, which gave the impression, at once, that he and they belonged to that ordinary, matter-of-fact class, among whom we were accustomed to see the domestic relations so naturally stand intact, that the idea of the breaking up of such a family by anything but death, never used to occur to us. I was therefore much surprised in being told by him that he had received intimations from a friend in Illinois to the effect that his wife was likely to seek a divorce from him. He for awhile appeared to feel deeply pained and mortified by the position of things; but, as time passed, he seemed to care less; and when, after a number of months, he announced that she had done as was predicted, there were no signs of a broken heart. Indeed after hearing the man talk on the subject several times, and seeing the light in which he viewed things, I came to doubt much whether California was in any way responsible for the event. Shallow, weak natures in whom selfishness predominates do not furnish depth of soil for the growth of life-long affection, or of the patient endurance that is faithful to sacred ties, even when suffering from coldness and neglect. But then, California had furnished the occasion of this estrangement and final separation; so of course California was blamed for it, as also, for various other similar events. Hints were sometimes heard in conversation, and occasionally appeared in newspaper paragraphs, to the effect that single men were proving a dangerous element in society, by insinuating themselves into the affections of married women, and, in some cases, supplanting husbands. I saw no instance of this kind myself until several years later, but I suppose some such must have existed, or I should not have seen a reply to those charges, which appeared as a communication in a California paper published long ago. The writer signed himself "A Bachelor." He premised that he was not moved to write the article by any wish, or necessity, to defend himself. His name was ready for anyone who chose to inquire for it; and he challenged the world to produce a single charge against his moral character. But, he claimed that as a bachelor, he stood in a position to see some things in a clearer light than most married men saw them; indeed to see things, that it appeared to him, some married men never saw at all. "We bachelors," he went on to say, "some of us at least, are not single because we have no appreciation of domestic life, or of the worth of a good woman. The causes that have led to our loneliness are various, often involving disappointments and sufferings the memory of which makes us look with keen interest on those who are enjoying a relationship that appears to us the best this life affords. We do not wish to pry into anybody's sanctum, but there are expressions of countenance, tones of voice, unconscious movements, habitual manners, that show, unerringly, what is in the heart of husband and wife towards each other. When into our boarding house, where, for many dreary California months we had seen no woman save our worthy widowed hostess, with silvered hair, there comes a gentleman and his wife fresh from the far east, we cannot help seeing their bearing one to the other; we cannot help feeling the atmosphere they carry about them. He engages in business, and, of course, must be absent from her most of the day. She busies herself with her two children—we see little of her—only hear her voice talking or singing to them, except that occasionally she sits with our landlady in the common sitting room when we are waiting to be called to dinner. She is near the window, and we see her face light up with a smile that looks to us divine. Unconsciously, she rises, with her youngest child on her arm, and is at the door when her husband enters. He scarcely smiles, looks beyond her, bows to the others in the room, then, bethinking himself, takes the child mechanically in his arms, sits down and begins talking to Mr. Dives about business;

while the child finding it cold there, struggles down and creeps to its mother. At another time she enters the room after he has come; her face kindles, she sits down by him, and in the most natural, genial way, begins to tell him of something that has transpired in social life, or in their own little family. It may be a trifle, but her woman's heart and woman's fancy invests it with a charm that to a dull bachelor seems very fascinating. Her husband occasionally says, 'Ah,' or 'Well,' maybe he makes a few words of reply, with now and then a cold smile; but is ready with instant animation to talk about politics or business with Mr. Dives. Similar things occur every day. We wonder that she is not out of all patience, or provoked to show resentment; but she is not. There has been an expression of intense pain and disappointment in her face many times, but the quickness with which she has conquered it, shows that she would rather die than have anybody see it. It is evident that she loves him with all her heart, and as my friend Jack, a brother bachelor, generous, impulsive and full of chivalrous ideas of woman and her worth, follows me to my room and closes the door, his face blazing with indignation, can you wonder gentlemen,—you married gentlemen,—if he hisses through his teeth, 'That man's a fool, or a brute!'

"They begin housekeeping in our neighborhood. He is more and more away from home, more and more absorbed in business. She has no mother, no sister, no old friend to speak to her. She devotes herself to her children. There are but few women to be acquainted with, fewer whose companionship she could enjoy; and those few she shrinks from, because she knows if she admits them as friends they must see her neglected life and guess her suffering heart, and she is proud, with the pride of an intensely sensitive nature. But our motherly hostess runs in to see the little family occasionally; and, as Jack and I are her oldest boarders—she used to call us her boys when she had no one here but her own son and us;—she cannot resist telling us of the loneliness and even privation that she finds at our neighbor's. She says she thinks he leaves her enough money when he goes away on business, as he does sometimes for a week or two together, to buy what she needs for food, but someone has called for rent a time or two when our old friend has been there; and besides this, she has scarcely any wood cut, and is unable to hire a man to cut it. Jack cannot stand this.

He takes a Magazine for an excuse and calls at our neighbor's. He offers to read her a story while she works. It is a short one. He begins a romp with her oldest girl; runs after her to the back door; discovers the small wood pile, suddenly bethinks him that a little exercise will do him good, and soon has two or three armfuls of wood ready for the stove. *I need not continue the story farther, though it has continued itself now for some months.* Jack's thoughts of her are pure and good. He says she is to him an angel; but he will not see her suffer alone. God forbid that I should apologize for wrong-doing, or withhold a word of warning from a friend in peril; but I write this article because I have reason to think that similar cases to this I have described exist in other places in California, and that when, in some instances, ruin and misery have resulted, the blame has been laid entirely to the charge of 'intriguing bachelors.' I do not believe that in this case it will so result, for Jack has too high an ideal of the woman he almost worships, and she's fortified by that 'Great Presence on the battlefield' which sustains every Christian soldier. But gentlemen, married gentlemen of California I want to ask you a question.[10] If, in such a case, broken hearts and ruined lives are the result, in the name of our common humanity with all its sympathies and its weaknesses, whose fault is it?"[11]

"Bachelor" was evidently in earnest—perhaps too much excited,—maybe a little one-sided, but when I read his article I hoped it would be read by many married men, and that they would have the good sense to take a look, for a few minutes, from a bachelor's point of view.

[Three and a half pages have been removed from the original manuscript at this point in the text. A note on the back of page 93 of Sarah Royce's handwritten manuscript reads: "The remainder of page 93, also pages 94, 95 & 96 are cut out of this manuscript." Beneath this is an accompanying note that reads: "The above is the hand writing of Ruth Royce, youngest daughter of Sarah Eleanor Royce. M. J. Compton"][12]

But, in the domestic life of those early days, it was not always the husband that was neglectful and indifferent nor the wife that was faithful. I knew a woman whose every need was richly supplied, her every wish kindly considered by her husband, and, whenever within his means, gratified. He built, as soon as his business allowed, one of the best dwellings to be found in the city where they lived. All was planned according to her directions, and modified to suit her whims. Yet, she was never contented. Pleasant words and smiles rarely greeted him. Imperious demands, and cold criticism embittered his life. He bore it patiently, and meant to keep on enduring for the sake of those sacred laws to which he ever acknowledged unswerving allegiance. But she contrived in some way, I never knew how, to get possession of a large portion of his property; and then to obtain a divorce. There must have been sad corruption somewhere; or she could never have carried it through.

Another instance of woman's unfaithfulness, came painfully under my notice. Her three children were, for some time, my pupils; the oldest, a girl just entering her teens, was rather remarkable for her good sense and womanly stability. The mother must have married early, for she was still young and quite handsome. The father was a man of good sense, average intelligence, and manners by no means disagreeable. Their home, whenever I saw it, seemed well furnished with comforts. But the fatal gift of beauty which the mother possessed, accompanied as it was by a weak vanity, laid her open to the flattery of the designing; and within two years of the time when I first knew them, the saddened father was left with no one but his thirteen-year-old girl to manage his forlorn household. Then there was Mrs. D——. How beautiful she was; so beautiful that when I first saw her it was difficult to remove my eyes from her face. If it had only been a picture on which I could look long without offence. But then, it was the *life* that made the chief charm; and I could not wonder at the evident admiration with which a remarkably fascinating neighbor of ours regarded her. But when that neighbor became more and more frequently her companion in her walks, as she passed by our retired nook, I sighed, not only for her sake and her husband's but for their three little girls. The end came rather slowly; but it came at last. She, herself in the paroxysms of a terrible illness, told her husband of her own fall; and of her repugnance to him; and he, with shame and pain, took those three little girls to his mother and sisters in the far east, never to see their mother again. How can she bear to look back to their babyhood? How can she endure to think of the works *she* has wrought into the fabric of California social life?

But it is a relief to turn from these sad pictures to the memory of that flowery spring, in the beginning of which I first entered, what I then believed to be, the most lovely village in California. Every smoothly-rolling hill was dressed in bloom; and the flat land of the valley stretched like a gorgeous carpet from the center of the village far back toward the foot of a grand old mountain. The air was full of the songs of answering meadow-larks, occasionally enriched by a glee from the more retiring mocking-bird. It was virtually my first California spring; for the only one I had previously seen in the state was spent in San Francisco, where, while I saw and enjoyed the softly-smiling skies, the brilliant sunshine, the calmly-sleeping waters of the Bay, and the rolling hills beyond, still I could not be out among the grass and flowers; all I saw of spring was in the distance; and very soon the summer winds and fogs, peculiar to San Francisco, ended the season for much out of doors enjoyment. But in our pretty village, or rather just on its outskirts, as I was, I had only to open the doors, and grass, and flowers, and birds were all about me. Then, the children enjoyed it so much. The older one ran about, picking flowers and making play-houses, while the baby sat in her cradle, or her little chair near the door, crowing and laughing, and watching the other. Life can never be very lonely or dull to a mother who sees her children healthful and happy, and who has faith in the constant presence of the great and good One, her own Helper and Friend, and the Guardian of those little treasures for whom she gladly cares and toils.

Our pleasant village at that early day could scarcely be expected to own a church building; but there was a school house, and in it were held meetings, most of the time, on every alternate Sunday. The preaching was usually by Methodist ministers coming either from a neighboring town or from San Francisco. Sometimes a clergyman of the Cumberland Presbyterian denomination officiated. There was usually a fair congregation for the size of the place; and it is needless to say that those composing it were among the most intelligent and respectable people of the town. We had a little Sunday School; and considerable interest was shown in it by the ministers, as well as by some of the best educated people of the neighborhood. There was no formal church organization; as the members of the congregation and the workers in the Sunday School belonged to three or four different denominations. But, as they agreed on the great foundation facts and principles of Christianity, harmony seemed to prevail among them.

As the season advanced, surrounding colors changed. The green of the hills became flecked with faded spots, which gradually spread till nearly the whole surface was of a rich old-gold color, and the wild oats stood in their proud maturity, boasting their wealth. But when the breeze swept over them, they had to bow, and dance, and laugh in merry sparkles; while the ever-green oaks, which here and there waved their boughs slowly above them, seemed conscious of the superior dignity of their richly-dark robes. Wild flowers still added, here and there, a dash of color, and the pasturing herds, moving, or at rest, gave life to the scene.

One hot August afternoon, when I was, as usual, alone with the children, as I passed across our kitchen-dining-room, near the open front door, my eye was caught by a moving object on the ground outside, coming toward the house. I stopped to look. It was a creature covering a space which looked to me about the size of an eight-year-old boy's hand. In the center was a round, hairy body terminated by a projecting hairy head, while legs looking like slender, hairy fingers, with the knuckles well set up, strode on each side making fast time toward the house. I had never seen one before, but I had read of them, and knew it in an instant. It was a tarantula! The first thought was that it would get under the house. Then I could not find it. It might crawl through some opening up into the house; when and where I shuddered to think—as Mary's low bed, and baby's cradle, came into my mind. It might get to where the children were then playing not far from the house. These thoughts all flashed through me in an instant, and at the same time I sprang out of the back door, seized a short heavy chunk of wood, ran round the end of the house so as to intercept the creature's path, and dropped the weapon directly upon it. I had literally crushed the enemy; but I could not for some time get over a constant impulse to scan closely the whole premises, and peer into every corner and aperture. However, I never saw another tarantula near the house, and a friend to whom I showed the remains, and who had been familiar with the creatures, both here and in Mexico, said it was unusual for them to be seen except in very undisturbed places. He also assured me that it was, really, a decidedly large specimen; and I got credit for having conquered a formidable foe, for, he said, if I had struck it with a stick and not at once disabled it, it would most likely have sprung at me. He had seen Mexican boys tease them in this way before killing them; and the boys had to be quick in their motions to escape being bitten.

The season rolled on, and brought the kindly, spring-like winter, with just enough of rain and storm to water well the earth, brighten the whole landscape, and make the sunny intervals seem like days come out of Paradise. Then another spring spread its verdant mantle, strewed its gorgeous flowers, scattered their fragrance into our faces till we were almost intoxicated with delight, won us out to walk and ride among its beauties, then made way for another rich, luxurious summer, which in its turn faded into a pensive autumn, whose air seemed full of mournful yet tender prophecies, and still I lived in that same little village. As I look back to the months I spent there, it always seems to me that there was then granted to me an extra installment of youth; so unexpectedly rich and fresh were the experiences that came to me during that time. Not that I was rich in worldly goods, nor in surroundings that are ordinarily supposed to make life happy. But there are spiritual treasures, experiences of heart and mind, the joy of having done good to some struggling soul, the gladness of witnessing and sharing victory over evil, the certainty of a Guiding Presence, always near;—these things bring a delight to the spirit which never comes from mere outward prosperity.

About the middle of that fall I again journied toward the interior of the State. But by this time the face of things was much changed. We went to live in a little mining town, not in the mountains as before, but on a river, within about twenty miles of Sacramento City. The sands of the river-bed were said to be rich in gold, which, of course, could only be washed out while the bed was dry, in the summer. But, besides this, gold had been discovered in the bluffs and banks on the north side of the stream; and, for washing this out, a large supply of water was needed. A number of San Francisco gentlemen had organized themselves into a company to meet this want. Their plan was to dam the river some distance above the bar, raise the water, by means of a steam engine, to the required height, run it through a large flume back of the diggings, and enough above them to give a sufficient fall, then sell the water to the miners, by the square inch, distributing it by means of small flumes as it was required. The necessary buildings were erected, the steam engine constructed, the great flume built, the whole involving an enormous expense; and while this was being done there was a gathering of miners,—among them a very few families. Tents and cloth houses were put up, occasionally a shanty, half logs and half boards, and one or two very inferior board houses. We located ourselves upon a very pretty spot on the bluff, within the shadow of two or three thrifty young oaks, and having on each side of us clusters of clean shrubbery, almost as pretty as a cultivated hedge, making for us a kind of enclosure. Our house was of cloth; but the frame of it was excellent; as was proved, within a few weeks after we entered it, by one of the longest and most terrific gales I ever experienced in California, accompanied by very heavy rain. For three days and nights did the floods descend and the winds beat. Our timbers bent, till the whole frail tenement seemed stooping under the strain; but, by a kind Providence, it weathered the blast; and, though there was some leakage in two or three places, we were on the whole tolerably comfortable, and the thing which I most dreaded,—bad colds for the children,—did not occur. Our house was not very large; but I contrived to make-believe quite an imposing establishment. In the first place I covered the floor entirely; partly with matting, partly with dark carpeting. One end I curtained off for a bedroom, and by having a trundle bed for the two older children (I had three now), I managed to make room for hanging up clothing, and for standing trunks. The rest of the house I divided,—more by the arrangement of the furniture than by actual partition,—into kitchen, dining-room, and parlor. The cook-stove, wood-box, and a cupboard, which I made with my own hands from a dry-goods box, about covered the space that I could conscientiously call kitchen. My dining room was not much larger; and was furnished with a table and a couple of chairs; and if I did have to use my dining table in preparing my bread, pies and cakes on baking days,

I did not have very far to go to put them into the oven, nor much farther, to put them in the cupboard, when done and cooled.

But the parlor,—that was my pride. There was against the wall a small table covered with a cloth, and holding a knick-knack or two, and a few choice books. Above it was a narrow shelf with some other books, and some papers. There were two or three plush-covered seats, which Mary and I called "ottomans." Their frames were rough boxes, which I had stuffed and covered myself. The rocking chair, when not required near the stove for baby, was always set in the parlor beside the table, suggesting leisure and ease; but the pride of all was my Melodeon [a small reed organ]. It was said to be the first one that was ever brought to California. It came round the Horn, had been used for a year or two in a Church in Sacramento; and now was, by unusual good fortune, mine. One of the "ottomans" answered for a music stool. There was little time for music during the day, except on Sundays; but at night when the children were all in bed, and the store,—for we had a store again,—kept my husband away; I used often to indulge myself in the melodies and harmonies that brought to me the most precious memories of earth and opened up visions of heaven; and then those bare rafters, and cloth walls became, for the time, a banquet-hall, and a cathedral.

But our life in this locality was short, for it turned out in a few months, that the expenses of the Water Company were so great, they could not let the miners have water without charging so high as to take nearly all that could be made by mining. They had meetings, and tried to make compromises, but the San Francisco capitalists showed that the enormous sums they had invested, and the necessary expenses of running the engine, made it impossible for them to furnish water at the rates the miners required; while the miners demonstrated as clearly that to pay for water at the Company's rates was ruinous to them. So, after two or three meetings, in which some rather stormy, and many quite pathetic speeches were made, depicting the sad disappointments of the great men who had built the great works, the parties parted. The next morning there appeared in monstrous, white, chalked letters, on the side of the big flume, the words, "Dried Up," evidently put there by some waggish miner, as his farewell. Soon, tents were struck, houses taken down, store broken up, and the once busy mining "Bar" was almost deserted. We heard afterward that wiser heads planned and executed the simple contrivance of a ditch tapping the river several miles above; and so conducting water by its own natural force, instead of expensive machinery, through a large area of moderately rich surface diggings. In this way a great deal of profitable mining was done for years afterward, on this very ground where the great failure occurred.

Early in the morning of a very hot day in early summer, our little family were once more seated in a well packed wagon,—to be followed by another one,—and the horses' heads were turned toward the Sierras. Not that we intended to ascend the mountains. Our destination was another mining camp, some miles up, in the foot hills. The intention was to seek a favorable spot near the said mining camp, which was a very flourishing town, settle upon the ground, claim it as a homestead, and make a family residence of it; while business might be carried on in the town. A pretty spot within a mile of the camp had been decided upon previous to our removal, as a good place to pitch our tent, and there we stopped at the end of that hot day. When, the next morning, we examined our surroundings everything looked so favorable it was decided to remain, while farther investigation was made as to the opening for business in the village. This latter prospect was found good; but it soon turned out that the place where we were staying was already claimed by a party who had begun improvements a little distance off. So, after a few days of prospecting, it was determined to make a claim farther from the mining town on the main road from Sacramento to the mountains. Accordingly a man or two set to work and reared our cloth house, which had been brought, with the frame, from our late place of abode. It was put up in a little grove of quite young, and rather slender oak trees, which, when the sun shone, threw their shadows on the white, transparent walls so distinctly that when inside with the door shut, one could almost trace out the leaves on the canvas. A few feet from the house, on one side, was a group of bushes, growing in such a way as to form almost a semi circle; while two or three young oaks, growing among them threw a grateful shade over the almost inclosed spot. With a bit of awning stretched over the least sheltered side, and a few yards of cloth tacked from one tree to another on the side toward the road, a delightful kitchen was at once improvised. Here our cook-stove was set up, and our cupboard placed on a box to raise it from the ground, then fastened firmly to a tree, our dining table and a few seats arranged at a little distance, and, at once, we had not only kitchen, but dining-room; pleasanter, for the season and situation, than in-door rooms could be. This gave me the whole inside of my house for bed-room and parlor, so that my establishment was now quite aristocratic.

When I had once more spread my carpeting and arranged my furniture, I sat down to my Melodeon* and made the woods and the pretty little hills ring with some of my favorite songs, while the two older children, delighted with their new surroundings, decked a play-house with acorns and wild flowers; and baby, in the large square box I had carpeted and lined for her, alternately peeped over its sides at them and me, or pulled herself up by her little fingers, which could nicely reach its edge, and crowed with delight at this newly found power.

Our house was several rods back from the road, and so, out of the dust, while, being on a gentle elevation we had a full view of all passers-by, whether riding or walking. It was a beautiful spot but lonely; for the nearest house one way was a half mile, in the other direction, still farther. The new arrangement in business caused me to be left much alone with the children. In the bright sunny days, while they played about me, and I was busied with household cares or sewing, I never felt lonely, at least not in a dreary way, and, even in the evening reading or writing would so occupy my mind as to keep me from timid apprehensions. But when, by and by, journeys to Sacramento, or up into the mountains caused me to be sometimes left alone, all night, it did seem a little dangerous. There were a few Indians in the vicinity, two or three of whom had once or twice straggled by, and paused to gaze, with some curiosity. But they were not formidable, and I would not allow myself to care much about them. When however one hot afternoon, two men came from the road for a drink of

*The small reed organ mentioned earlier.

water, one of them an English sailor, not prepossessing in appearance, the other a foreigner—who the English man said came from Malacca—having one of the most ferociously savage-looking faces I ever saw; I did become decidedly nervous. They took their drink and did not stay long; but I could not keep that horrid face out of my mind long together, and every time I thought of it, a sense of the utter defenselessness of my position would force itself upon me. I knew I was to be alone that night, and as evening approached, I grew more and more wary and sensitive to every sound; till by the time the children were in bed and asleep I felt as if I should never be sleepy again. I had, before dusk, made everything as snug as possible in our out-door apartment and now, putting out my light, that it might not attract notice, I prepared to act as watchman for the night.

I had made, for the hot weather, two windows in our house. This was done by ripping, in the vertical seams of the cloth wall, a space of about eighteen or twenty inches in length, then rolling back the two edges away from each other, right and left and pinning them midway of the open space, so making a diamond shaped window. One of the windows was by the side of the front door, the other looked out toward the kitchen. Whenever I wished to close them I took out the pins, when the edges pulled themselves together, and the canvas being elastic enough for me to lap them a little, I could, by using pins sufficient, make them nearly as secure as if sewed.

On this night of my lonely watch, I let the edges fall together, that no dark space might be seen from outside, then took my station at the window beside the front door. By placing a finger or two in the bottom of the slit I could plainly see the whole space between the trees from the house to the road. It was bright moonlight and all looked so beautiful and peaceful that I felt soothed, and pleasant, sacred thoughts relieved my anxiety; but I did not feel at all sleepy. I hummed, very softly, some sweet verses, in dear old tunes; and precious companionship seemed to gather about me. I was losing all sense of fear when a shrill, loud, long bark, ending in a prolonged howl, startled me. It was in the direction of the kitchen, and I went softly to the slit on that side, and peeped out. After a few moments of entire silence, there was a rustling in the bushes beyond the stove, and soon there appeared out of the shadows a full sized coyote. He walked all about our little enclosure, smelt at every box and bag, tried with his nose to open the cupboard and seemed for some time bent on depredation; but failing in finding anything to suit him, by and by he trotted off into the woods again. I returned to my seat at the front slit, again all alive to the least sound that might stir the air. After some time there was a little movement, at first so slight it might be just a faint breeze rising; but no, not a leaf stirred. The sound became regular,—it was a footstep,—it was approaching along the road from the direction those men had taken. Was there more than one? I could not tell— they might be keeping step together. The sound came nearer. In a moment I should see somebody come in sight. The step ceased; then the form of a man moved cautiously out from the shadow of the bushes and turned from the road towards the house. I scarcely breathed. In a few paces he stopped, stood perfectly motionless, and evidently listened; then turned toward the road again. Was he going to call his companion? No, he tended the other way; he reached the road, then walked directly on, passing straight by, and I heard his step keeping regular time till quite out of hearing. The tension of my nerves had been so great, the reaction was inexpressible. Still I kept my watch; but all remained quiet.

As that danger had passed so harmlessly why might I not relax my guard? It was getting towards morning—I would rest. So I lay down and slept till the sun was shining full on the front of the house. I dressed, and was nearly ready to go to my kitchen and prepare breakfast, when a quick step was heard coming up the path from the road straight to the house, and directly there was a tap on the framework of the door. I said, "Who's there?" and a laughing voice answered, giving the name of an old friend who once, for a while, was an inmate in our family when we lived down at the Bay. We were soon chatting sociably in the kitchen, and having breakfast with the children; while we enjoyed a hearty laugh, as it came out in conversation that it was he who had caused my almost breathless fear of the night before. He had, the day before, come by stage from Sacramento to a town six or seven miles from our place and, determining to visit us, had made some inquiries about the road; and started to walk it rather late in the day. It turned out to be farther than he had supposed; so that when he found himself in front of the house he knew it must be fully ten o'clock. He paused, and then walked a little towards the house thinking he might hear us talking,—but finding all still he determined to go on to the public house, which, having some previous knowledge of the neighborhood, he knew was about a half mile distant. So that supposed danger turned out to be no danger at all.

In two or three hours my husband came home, and for a few days I had plenty of company and protection. I played and sung old favorite pieces, we talked and walked, and one day ascended a high hill which I had often noticed with interest, as it was the only thing within sight of the house that looked like a mountain. But, in a few days—I was alone again—and I felt it worse than ever. One of my lonely nights soon after that, brought a little, bright incident, which I always like to recall. I had awakened in the middle of the night, which was very dark, to attend to some want of one of the children, and was just ready to lie down again when suddenly all was light as day. The branches and leaves of the trees threw their shadows on the canvas as in sunlight. I had time to think, "It is a fire! no, it is too white a light for that, it is a meteor!" when all was dark again. A day or two after when my husband came home, the papers he brought gave accounts of a remarkable meteor which was seen that very night passing over Sacramento and some of the foot hill towns. I so regretted not having seen the meteor itself; though the effects I did see, were I suppose almost as wonderful and certainly more unique.

Another dark night brought a less agreeable sensation. From a very sound sleep I was awakened by the tramp of horses, and at the same moment heard a man's voice, close by, say distinctly, "I know she's alone, for I saw her husband going away this morning and he said he would be gone two days." A creeping chill came over me. Another voice, lower and less distinct, replied. Then my name was called very emphatically. I answered as firmly as I could, and in what I meant should be a defiant tone. The first voice then said, "We didn't want to frighten you, but we are looking for a lost man, and we called to ask if you have heard anybody making any noise about here." I said "no," and asked further explanation. It seemed that two of the men at the neighboring public house had ridden, the preceding day, to town, and started for home in the evening. One of them had been drinking a good deal, and was restive about leaving town, urging the other to turn back with him. The other became tired of his obstinacy, and rode off, thinking his companion would follow when he found his entreaties vain. Late at night the horse of the drunken man came home without his rider; and the men who had so startled me, were out hunting for him. They passed on; but I did not soon go to sleep again. In about an hour I again heard horses' feet, and a voice called out in passing, "We've found him; he was lying by the road-side, all right."

Another threatened danger had thus turned out harmless to me; but this kind of incident was really far from agreeable; and as there seemed no probability that this claim would ever become an improved homestead; it was decided that I should move into the mining village two miles off. So in the early autumn I bade farewell to the canvas house and never saw it again. In town, we lived in a little frame cottage quite out of the crowd but near enough for protection. There were very few families; but two or three in the neighborhood, hearing my Melodeon, soon formed the habit of dropping in, on certain evenings of each week, to "have a sing" as they expressed it. By and by, a clergyman living a few miles off called on us, and we arranged an appointment for him to preach in our sitting room, which was probably as large as any room in town unless it were the bar-room of the tavern, down in the ravine. He had appointments in several places; so could only come once in two weeks; but that might be an opening for something better in the future. Though we had been told there was, among the miners, considerable sport made of the "psalm singing" at our house; yet there was a good congregation gathered there; enough at least to crowd the room pretty well; and tax the ingenuity of two or three to arrange seats for them. It was interesting to any thoughtful person in those days to observe the bearing of many, among even the roughest miners, towards those who they believed were in earnest in religion. They seemed to watch such persons with a look of mingled curiosity and respect, and appeared very generally to consider it desirable to have some of that sort among them.

But we had not an opportunity to hold many meetings there; for in the spring another removal was determined upon. This time it was to one of the largest and pleasantest of the mining towns quite high up in the Sierra Nevada Mountains; higher than Weaverville our first California dwelling place. Here we found ourselves at once in contact with a number of very good Christian people. There were three Churches, all very well attended, and each sustaining a Sunday School. There was also a good sized Public School, as well as one or two social and beneficent societies.

Here I seemed to have found, in one sense at least, a rest. For a little more than twelve years we lived in that Town, or so closely on its outskirts as to be always considered among its inhabitants. During that twelve years California passed through various periods of convulsion which seemed to threaten her welfare. Now it was the great Vigilance Committee movement of San Francisco, which was felt to the very tops of the Sierras. Then the Frazer River excitement drained most of her towns of many inhabitants. Again, the Washoe fever sent thousands surging wildly over the high ridges they had once dreaded to approach; while at almost the same time the awful roar of Civil War burst from cannons on the Atlantic Shore and rolled over every mountain and plain till it met the moaning surges of the Pacific. For awhile it threatened to set every man's hand against his brother; and banish prosperity from our homes. But after the storm there came a calm. Then the great Overland Rail Road became the theme of all tongues, and in due time it helped to carry prosperity to California as well as to the Interior. And so life has rolled on, not only for the twelve years of which I was speaking, but for many years since, and California as a State has rallied from numerous shocks, and is now smiling in prosperity; while her first adopted children many of them, have passed away; and those remaining have grown old, and look back on years of wonderful experiences which they sometimes wish could be recorded along with the history of their adopted State; for their children and their children's children to read, that they might learn to love and reverence the God who through all the devious paths of life ever guides safely those who trust and obey Him.

And now, to conclude, I have an incident to record which I think rather remarkable. On the 9th of September 1884, thirty four years from the day California was admitted into the Union, I was in San Francisco; and I walked to the same house which I first entered on the 19th of January 1850. I was met at the door by the gentleman who in 1849 built the house, and, who when I first entered it was busy finishing it; and being cordially recognized by him, we talked of those old times. I then, by his permission, ascended to the high veranda and stood upon the very spot where in October 1850 I had stood with another old Californian and had seen the Oregon come into port with "California Admitted" streaming at her mast head. Words are powerless to express the thoughts and emotions of one permitted, like myself at that moment, to step backward in time thirty four years.

In a country proverbial for the instability of all things, it is rare for persons and places, entirely separated for a generation of time, thus to come together again.

:·. ·:· ·:.

Appendix

A SARAH ROYCE TIMELINE

March 2, 1819	Sarah Bayliss is born in Stratford-upon-Avon, England. At three months she is brought to the United States. The family lives alternately in Germantown, Pennsylvania, and New York City.
1828	The Bayliss family moves to Rochester, New York.
early 1840	Sarah Bayliss graduates from Phipps Union Female Seminary in Albion, New York, and begins teaching school in Rochester.
May 31, 1845	Sarah Bayliss marries Josiah Royce.
November 23, 1846	Mary Eleanor is born.
Spring 1848	The Royces move to a village near Tipton, Iowa.
January 24, 1848	James W. Marshall discovers gold at Sutter's Fort.
April 30, 1849	The Royces leave for California.
August 4, 1849	The party crosses the Continental Divide.
October 12, 1849	The Royces start to cross the Sierra Nevada mountains.
October 19, 1849	The Royces cross the highest part of the mountain pass.
end of October 1849	The Royces make it to Weaverville, try panning for gold, and decide to open a grocery.

mid-December 1849	The Royces move to Sacramento.
January 9, 1850	The Sacramento River floods.
January 15, 1850	The Royces move to San Francisco, where they will reside for four years.
1850–1851	Sarah teaches school.
July 13, 1850	Harriette (Hattie) is born.
1851	The Royces move to a village near San Francisco, and Josiah takes up farming.
August 1852	John Samuel is born but dies shortly thereafter.
1852/1853	The Royces go back to the mines and open a store in a mining camp twenty miles from Sacramento.
Summer 1853	The Royces move to another mining camp.
September 21, 1853	Ruth is born.
spring 1854	The Royces move to Grass Valley, where they live for twelve years.
February 1855	Sarah opens a school in Grass Valley.
November 20, 1855	Josiah Jr. is born.
1857	Josiah Sr. and Thomas Barr buy the land that will become Avon Farm.
1857–1862	Sometime during this five-year period, the Royces move to Avon Farm. They live in a two-story white frame farmhouse that they share with Barr.
1862	The Royces sell their share of Avon Farm to Barr, although Sarah and the children continue to live in the farmhouse for a time.
1865	Royce is teaching in the public school at this time.
spring 1866	The Royces move back to San Francisco and run a fruit store.
1870	The Royces move across the bay from San Francisco to the village of Brooklyn. Josiah Jr. enters college at the University

	of California at Oakland at fifteen years of age.
1873	The Royces move into Oakland proper.
1870s	The Royces move to various homes around Oakland, driven by economic factors related to Josiah Sr.'s declining health.
1884–1886	Sarah writes "Across the Plains" at Josiah Jr.'s request.
1886	Josiah Jr.'s history of California is published by Houghton, Mifflin and Company.
June 23, 1888	Josiah Sr. dies of a stroke in Los Gatos, California.
1888	Sarah moves in with Ruth in San Jose.
November 24, 1891	Sarah Royce dies.
1932	Yale University Press publishes Sarah Royce's story as *A Frontier Lady*.

·:· ·:· ·:·
Notes

Introduction

1. Royce, Sarah Eleanor. "Across the Plains." Sarah Royce reminiscences. Ms. 72/53 c. Bancroft Library. U of California, Berkeley, 2. Further citations to "Across the Plains" are given in parentheses in the text.

2. Kevin Starr's claims about female fortitude in California are a common portrayal of Royce. See *Americans and the California Dream, 1850–1915*. New York: Oxford UP, 1973. 359.

3. Wrobel, David M. *Promised Lands: Promotion, Memory, and the Creation of the American West*. Lawrence: UP of Kansas, 2002. 4.

4. Wrobel, 13.

5. Johnson, Susan Lee. *Roaring Camp: The Social World of the California Gold Rush*. New York: W. W. Norton, 2000. 26.

6. Johnson, 27.

7. Johnson, Susan Lee. "'A memory sweet to soldiers': The Significance of Gender in the History of the 'American West.'" *Western Historical Quarterly* 24 (November 1993): 495–517. 499.

8. In his biography of Josiah Royce, John Clendenning describes the religious zeal that characterized the upstate New York region during the first half of the nineteenth century. Clendenning also provides helpful information about Sarah Royce's early years. See Clendenning, John. *The Life and Thought of Josiah Royce*. Madison: U of Wisconsin P, 1985. 6–11.

9. See Clendenning, John. *The Letters of Josiah Royce*. Chicago: U of Chicago P, 1970. 12. Also see Hine, Robert V. *Josiah Royce: From Grass Valley to Harvard*. Norman: U of Oklahoma P, 1992. 26.

10. Hine, 193.

11. Ibid., 17.

12. Ibid., 5.

13. Clendenning, 13.

14. Buranelli, Vincent. *Josiah Royce*. New York: Twayne Publishers, 1964. 51.

15. Brian Roberts argues that the moral sensibilities of Royce and other "respectable women" were at odds with the male-dominated society of Gold

Rush California. See Roberts, Brian. *American Alchemy: The California Gold Rush and Middle-Class Culture.* Chapel Hill: U of North Carolina P, 2000. 255.

16. See Ralph Henry Gabriel's "Concerning the Manuscript of Sarah Royce" in Royce, Sarah. *A Frontier Lady: Recollections of the Gold Rush and Early California.* Ed. Ralph Henry Gabriel. Yale UP, 1932. Lincoln: U of Nebraska P, 1997.

17. See Brown, Dee. *The Gentle Tamers: Women of the Old Wild West.* New York: Putnam, 1958. Joan M. Jensen and Darlis A. Miller take on Brown's depiction of women in their 1980 article "Gentle Tamers Revisited: New Approaches to the History of Women in the American West." *Pacific Historical Review* 49:2 (1980): 459–62. Deborah Lawrence claims, "Brown's depiction of white women as harbingers of civilization continues to dominate literature and classroom" (133, note 3). See Lawrence, Deborah. *Writing the Trail: Five Women's Frontier Narratives.* Iowa City: U of Iowa P, 2006.

18. Works such as the essays in *Women and Gender in the American West* (eds. Mary Ann Irwin and James F. Brooks. Albuquerque: U of New Mexico P, 2004) and Cathryn Halverson's *Maverick Autobiographies* (Madison: U of Wisconsin P, 2004) explore new visions of western women's experiences from historical and literary critical perspectives.

19. Swetnam, Susan H. "A New Day in the Study of Western Women's Experience: Who'll Follow?" *Western American Literature* 42:2 (Summer 2007): 189–196. 190.

20. Ibid., 190.

21. Butler, Anne M. "The Way We Were, the Way We Are, and the Way Ahead." *Western Historical Quarterly* 36 (Winter 2005): 423–427. 425.

22. A good example of this is Deborah Lawrence's claim about Royce's choice in entitling her final chapter "Fortitude" (58).

23. Royce, Josiah. *California, From the Conquest in 1846 to the Second Vigilance Committee in San Francisco.* Boston: Houghton Mifflin, 1886. Josiah Royce discusses his mother's manuscript on pages 241–246 and 403–406.

24. Kowalewski, Michael. "Romancing the Gold Rush: The Literature of the California Frontier." *Rooted in Barbarous Soil: People, Culture, and Community in Gold Rush California.* Ed. Kevin Starr and Richard J. Orsi. Berkeley: U of California P, 2000. 206.

25. Royce, Josiah. 1.

26. Starr, Kevin. *Americans and the California Dream, 1850–1915.* New York: Oxford UP, 1973. 155.

27. Ibid., 142.

28. I base this conjecture on Royce's background as an educated woman and the characteristics that can be gleaned from understanding her as she portrays herself in her narrative: as an intelligent and considered person.

29. Sarah Royce's diary does not accompany the manuscript of Royce's narrative, which is held in the Bancroft Library at the University

of California, Berkeley. It is also not listed in the finding aids for the
Josiah Royce Memorial Collection, held in the University of California,
Los Angeles, archives or the Josiah Royce materials held in the Harvard
University archives.

30. Georgi-Findlay, Brigitte. *The Frontiers of Women's Writing: Women's
Narratives and the Rhetoric of Westward Expansion*. Tucson: U of Arizona
P, 1996. 108.

31. Lewis, Nathaniel. *Unsettling the Literary West: Authenticity and
Authorship*. Lincoln: U of Nebraska P, 2003. 20.

32. Ibid., 9.

33. Ibid., 9.

34. Lewis, 31.

35. Turner, Victor. *Dramas, Fields, and Metaphors: Symbolic Action in
Human Society*. Ithaca: Cornell UP, 1974. 232.

36. Lawrence comments on the liminal position of Royce herself, 130.

37. Lawrence mentions travelers' urge to record their names on
Independence Rock, 45.

38. Kaplan, Amy. "Manifest Domesticity." *No More Separate Spheres: A
Next Wave American Studies Reader*. Ed. Cathy N. Davidson and Jessamyn
Hatcher. Durham: Duke UP, 2002. 186.

39. Ibid., 190.

40. Lawrence, 40.

41. Wrobel, 185.

42. Wilson, Luzena Stanley. *My Checkered Life: Luzena Stanley
Wilson in Early California*. Ed. Fern Henry. Nevada City, CA: Carl Mautz
Publishing, 2003. 32.

43. Ibid., 63.

44. This may be a function of the requests to tell their stories about their
overland journey and experiences in California.

45. Wilson, 14.

46. Ibid., 12–13.

47. Ibid., 13.

48. Ibid., 57.

49. Ibid., 113.

50. Ibid., 112.

51. Ibid., 129.

52. Ibid., 130.

53. Ibid., 130.

54. Hine, 137.

55. According to the Nevada Humanities Committee Web site, Doris
Dwyer had portrayed Sarah Royce in Chautauqua performances. See
"Biographies of Chautauqua Performers." *Nevada Humanities*. 21 June
2006. 12 December 2006.

<http://www.nevadahumanities.org/chautauqua/performers.htm>.
Sarah Royce's narrative is excerpted in a textbook for children in

grades 5–8. See Shuter, Jane. Ed. *Sarah Royce and the American West.*
Raintree Steck-Vaughn Publishers, 1996.

56. The Nevada County Library in Nevada City, California, includes images of three pages from Sarah Royce's handwritten manuscript on their Web site. See "Sarah Royce Manuscript 'Across the Plains.'" *Nevada County Library.* 2005. 12 December 2006. <http://new.mynevadacounty.com/library/index.cfm?ccs=1048&cs=1166>.

57. Wrobel, 127.

Across the Plains

1. The Royces had been living in Tipton, Iowa, which is approximately 270 miles east of Council Bluffs.

2. The Genesee River flows through Rochester, New York, where Royce had lived with her parents and where she met and married her husband, Josiah.

3. Timing was important for travelers on the Overland Trail, as they needed to cross the Sierra Nevada range before the heavy snowfall of winter sealed off the entrance into California until the snow melted in spring. The story of the ill-fated Donner Party, stranded in the Sierras in the winter of 1846–47, would have been fresh in the minds of those making the journey.

4. I Samuel 7:12: "Then Samuel took a stone, and set it between Mizpeh and Shen, and called the name of it Eben-ezer, saying, Hitherto hath the LORD helped us."

5. Genesis 21:16: "And she went, and sat her down over against him a good way off, as it were a bowshot: for she said, Let me not see the death of the child. And she sat over against him, and lift up her voice, and wept." Genesis chapter 21 tells the story of Hagar.

6. Exodus 3:1: "Now Moses kept the flock of Jethro his father in law, the priest of Midian: and he led the flock to the backside of the desert, and came to the mountain of God, even to Horeb." And Exodus 17:6: "Behold, I will stand before thee there upon the rock in Horeb; and thou shalt smite the rock, and there shall come water out of it, that the people may drink. And Moses did so in the sight of the elders of Israel."

7. The California census for 1849 reported only 8 percent of the population to be women. However, Jo Ann Levy claims that figures would actually have been higher because "some tabulators ignored prostitutes." See Jo Ann Levy, *They Saw the Elephant: Women in the California Gold Rush.* Norman: U of Oklahoma P, 1992. 176–177.

8. Luzena Stanley Wilson includes descriptions of the flood in her memoirs that are remarkably similar to Royce's and the experiences Royce depicts. See Wilson, Luzena Stanley. *My Checkered Life: Luzena Stanley Wilson in Early California.* Ed. Fern Henry. Nevada City, CA: Carl Mautz Publishing, 2003.

9. Levy identifies "Irene" as Irene McCready, a well-known prostitute in San Francisco. 169.

10. Royce originally wrote "Gentlemen of Calif," then erased "of Calif" and wrote the word "married" instead. The fact that she changed her wording here suggests that, in retelling this story, she wished to emphasize that she was addressing the married rather than the unmarried men.

11. Royce writes the words "Whose fault is it?" larger than that the rest of her writing on the page in order to emphasize this point.

12. The contents of these excised pages are unknown.

Bibliography

Archives and Collections

Royce, Josiah, Memorial Collection, 1875–1936. Special Collections, University of California, Los Angeles.

Royce, Josiah, Papers, 1855–1944. Harvard University Archives.

Royce, Sarah. Bancroft Library, University of California, Berkeley.

Published Works

Brown, Dee. *The Gentle Tamers: Women of the Old Wild West.* New York: Putnam, 1958.

Buranelli, Vincent. *Josiah Royce.* New York: Twayne Publishers, 1964.

Butler, Anne M. "The Way We Were, the Way We Are, and the Way Ahead." *Western Historical Quarterly* 36 (Winter 2005): 423–427.

Clendenning, John. *The Letters of Josiah Royce.* Chicago: U of Chicago P, 1970.

———. *The Life and Thought of Josiah Royce.* Madison: U of Wisconsin P, 1985.

Gabriel, Ralph Henry. "Concerning the Manuscript of Sarah Royce." *A Frontier Lady: Recollections of the Gold Rush and Early California.* By Sarah Royce. Yale UP, 1932. Lincoln: U of Nebraska P, 1997.

Georgi-Findlay, Brigitte. *The Frontiers of Women's Writing: Women's Narratives and the Rhetoric of Westward Expansion.* Tucson: U of Arizona P, 1996.

Halverson, Cathryn. *Maverick Autobiographies.* Madison: U of Wisconsin P, 2004.

Hine, Robert V. *Josiah Royce: From Grass Valley to Harvard.* Norman: U of Oklahoma P, 1992.

Irwin, Mary Ann, and James F. Brooks, eds. *Women and Gender in the American West.* Albuquerque: U of New Mexico P, 2004.

Jensen, Joan M., and Darlis A. Miller. "Gentle Tamers Revisited: New Approaches to the History of Women in the American West." *Pacific Historical Review* 49:2 (1980): 173–213.

Johnson, Susan Lee. "'A memory sweet to soldiers': The Significance of Gender in the History of the 'American West.'" *Western Historical Quarterly* 24 (November 1993): 495–517.

———. *Roaring Camp: The Social World of the California Gold Rush.* New York: W. W. Norton, 2000.

Kaplan, Amy. "Manifest Domesticity." *No More Separate Spheres: A Next Wave American Studies Reader.* Eds. Cathy N. Davidson and Jessamyn Hatcher. Durham: Duke UP, 2002.

Kowalewski, Michael. "Romancing the Gold Rush: The Literature of the California Frontier." *Rooted in Barbarous Soil: People, Culture, and Community in Gold Rush California.* Eds. Kevin Starr and Richard J. Orsi. Berkeley: U of California P, 2000.

Lawrence, Deborah. *Writing the Trail: Five Women's Frontier Narratives.* Iowa City: U of Iowa P, 2006.

Lewis, Nathaniel. *Unsettling the Literary West: Authenticity and Authorship.* Lincoln: U of Nebraska P, 2003.

Nevada Humanities Committee. "Biographies of Chautauqua Performers." *Nevada Humanities.* 21 June 2006. 12 December 2006. <http://www.nevadahumanities.org/chautauqua/performers.htm>.

Roberts, Brian. *American Alchemy: The California Gold Rush and Middle-Class Culture.* Chapel Hill: U of North Carolina P, 2000.

Royce, Josiah. *California, From the Conquest in 1846 to the Second Vigilance Committee in San Francisco.* Boston: Houghton Mifflin, 1886.

Royce, Sarah Eleanor. "Across the Plains." Sarah Royce reminiscences. Ms. 72/53 c. Bancroft Library. U of California, Berkeley.

"Sarah Royce Manuscript 'Across the Plains.'" *Nevada County Library.* 2005. 12 December 2006. <http://new.mynevadacounty.com/library/index.cfm?ccs=1048&cs=1166>.

Shuter, Jane, ed. *Sarah Royce and the American West.* Raintree Steck-Vaughn Publishers, 1996.

Starr, Kevin. *Americans and the California Dream, 1850–1915.* New York: Oxford UP, 1973.

Swetnam, Susan H. "A New Day in the Study of Western Women's Experience: Who'll Follow?" *Western American Literature* 42:2 (Summer 2007): 189–196.

Turner, Victor. *Dramas, Fields, and Metaphors: Symbolic Action in Human Society.* Ithaca: Cornell UP, 1974. 232.

Wilson, Luzena Stanley. *My Checkered Life: Luzena Stanley Wilson in Early California.* Ed. Fern Henry. Nevada City, CA: Carl Mautz Publishing, 2003.

Wrobel, David M. *Promised Lands: Promotion, Memory, and the Creation of the American West.* Lawrence: UP of Kansas, 2002.

Index

‎∴‎ ∴‎ ∴‎
About the Author

Jennifer Dawes Adkison is an associate professor of English at Idaho State University. She has published essays on depictions of western women in contemporary novels and on the nineteenth-century nature writer Susan Fenimore Cooper. She received her PhD in 2001 from University of Nevada, Reno, where she studied in the Literature and Environment Program.